An Essay on
King Lear

S. L. GOLDBERG

*Robert Wallace Professor of English
University of Melbourne*

CAMBRIDGE UNIVERSITY PRESS

Cambridge
London   New York   New Rochelle
Melbourne   Sydney

Published by the Press Syndicate of the University of Cambridge
The Pitt Building, Trumpington Street, Cambridge CB2 1RP
32 East 57th Street, New York, NY 10022, USA
296 Beaconsfield Parade, Middle Park, Melbourne 3206, Australia

© Cambridge University Press 1974

First published 1974
Reprinted 1980

Library of Congress catalogue card number: 73–84318

ISBN 0 521 20200 0 hard covers
ISBN 0 521 09831 9 paperback

First printed in Great Britain
by W & J Mackay Limited, Chatham
Reprinted in Great Britain at the
University Press, Cambridge

To
J.P.A.

Contents

Introduction

. . . we must obey;
Speak what we feel, not what we ought to say . . .
(v, iii, 323–4)

Anyone who sets out to say what he makes of *King Lear* is
soon likely to start wondering at his rashness. The further
he goes, the less easy he finds it even to keep his critical
balance. More perhaps than any other work – certainly
more than any other of Shakespeare's, I think – it impels us
finally to 'speak what we feel, not what we ought to say'.
To 'obey' it is to answer with nothing less. And yet it also
makes us feel that whatever we do speak, or could speak, is
inadequate to everything else we are brought to feel – even,
in some obscure way, a betrayal of it. The drama so engages
us that to feel it adequately requires us in the end to become
wholly open to, totally consumed in, the most painful and
bewildering feelings. But because those feelings press toward release, toward some form in which we can name them
and (to that extent at least) master them, to speak adequately requires us in the end to detach ourselves from our
feelings, to withhold or withdraw some part of ourselves
from the integrity with which we have to experience the
drama. It is a difficult enough predicament for any reader or
spectator; for the critic, who commits himself to expressing
some coherent sense of the play as a whole, it is acute –
and none the less so because (as I see it) this kind of predicament is largely what the play is about. It is hardly
surprising that many accounts of *King Lear* strike a tone that
somehow falsifies it. Some critics, for example, sound so ideal-
istic, so emotionally effusive, so eager to find confirmation

I

of their own values in it, that they seem to have missed how deeply and persistently the play is concerned to examine the nexus between values and personal feeling. Others sound so detached, so self-possessed, so 'objective', so fundamentally *un*disturbed in tone, that they seem to have missed how formidably the play questions such detachment and self-possession in the face of the human experience it gives us to witness and to share. Clearly, to speak about such experience justly is a peculiarly delicate business, and a peculiarly self-revealing one too; it is hard for anyone not to seem either too emotionally involved in it or too detached from it. To see the dangers is not necessarily to avoid them, and though I draw attention to them at the outset, it is not because I have much confidence that I avoid them myself. On the contrary; for it is part of my argument that probably nobody can.

As far as possible, I try to allow my argument to follow the logic of the play itself. I do so for two reasons. The first is simply that I cannot see any more adequate way of eliciting what the drama does make us feel, and why, nor any briefer yet still accurate way of stating it. The play is so tightly organized and so continuously self-qualifying that a reading of it can hardly avoid becoming close-knit and self-qualifying itself; and I should perhaps say at once that this essay is likely to disappoint the reader who wants of criticism a straightforward, clear-cut statement of a straightforward, clear-cut position. Extended as it is, my argument is conceived (as I hope it will be read) as a single whole. For although I believe *King Lear* has an integral meaning, I do not believe it consists in any easily formulable 'philosophy'. The play does not offer us anything like a single, straightforward, clear-cut attitude to life, or a guaranteed moral vantage-point, even if some of the characters in it seem to;

part of its integrity, I would argue, is precisely that it does not. But when so many people think that it does, or think that if it doesn't it should, it seems to me better to err on the side of cautious advance and minute explicitness than of bold, readily grasped assertion. In the area of Shakespearean tragedy – where the integrity of our deepest feelings and values is challenged by what they must also judge – prompt, business-like attitudes are likely to be only a source of darkness.

The second reason for trying to follow the 'logic' of the play is a more general one, and calls for some preliminary explanation.

To use a word like 'logic' is to imply that the play has a structure that exists in time – in other words, that the play cannot be adequately described in 'spatial' terms. I think this is the case. It is true of any play – indeed, of any literary work – but it also has a special relevance to this one.

That *King Lear* has a 'temporal' structure, an action, seems plain enough; and as far as I know, nobody has ever doubted it. What the action consists in, however, and why it is important, are another matter. In the post-Bradleyan excitements about 'spatial' and 'organic' kinds of structure in Shakespeare, it was generally argued that these were more basic, more essential, than the 'temporal' action. The latter, it was generally supposed, was merely what the characters did and suffered – more particularly, what the protagonist did and suffered, the sequence of events in which his character was gradually revealed as his fate. The action being regarded only as a function of character, and character only as a function of the poetry, both, it seemed, could be treated as secondary or even left aside: Bradley had taken them as far as they could go, and probably further. The analysis of imagery, themes, symbolism, the 'atmospheric' texture of the verse, was thought to discover a deeper and more significant kind of structure – the structure not of the protagonist's character, but of Shakespeare's own imaginative insight, his 'vision' of the world.

The curious result of this has been to leave Bradley's conception of the dramatic action pretty much in command of the field – and especially with *King Lear* (for it was implicitly questioned with other tragedies). Even now it is still generally assumed, for example, that the action of *Lear* is what Bradley thought it was: the pattern of deeds, of events – in this case, primarily spiritual events – issuing from Lear's character and issuing back into it. True, this pattern is supplemented by the story of Gloucester and of the other characters; but the meaning of the play as a whole, in so far as it is gradually revealed to our sight, is thought to lie chiefly in the actions and consciousness of its hero. Analysis of the play's 'organic' or 'spatial' structure, of its use of traditional beliefs and symbols, of the effect of theatrical conventions, has really left untouched two basic assumptions of Bradley's reading: that the drama moves in time only in order to represent the spiritual history of Lear; and secondly, that as we identify with the hero, so we identify the end of his spiritual history as the meaning of the drama. The play is commonly thought to represent a man moving from blindness and folly, through the bitter lessons of his consequent suffering, eventually to see the truth. Whether or not this truth withstands what the terrible final catastrophe does to his spirit may be debatable; it is perhaps nothing less than a mystery. But about the vehicle by which Shakespeare's meaning is conveyed to us, and where we must therefore look for the last particle of it, there is (so it would seem) little doubt: it is what he makes his hero come to 'see', the ultimate state to which he brings the hero's consciousness.

Neither this general conception of a dramatic action, nor

the usual view of *King Lear* based on it, seems to me wholly convincing. Clearly, they both contain more than a grain of truth; they would have collapsed very quickly if they didn't. But I think the general conception does nevertheless over-simplify the nature of dramatic 'character', and hence the relationship of the hero to everything else in the drama, hence our relationship to the hero, and finally, therefore, the connection between 'character', 'insight', and 'vision'. Applied to this play, where 'sight' and 'insight' are such crucial terms both for the characters and (in a somewhat different sense) for ourselves, such over-simplifications can become positively misleading. This is the reason for my rather theoretical digression in chapter 2; it is an attempt to clear the ground a little before trying to proceed. As for the usual view of *Lear*, it is in order to help clarify what I think the play's action does consist in, and why it is of central importance, that I try as far as possible to follow the play's own 'logic'.

For the usual reading does raise some awkward questions. How much does it matter, for example, that Cordelia has a touch of hard steel in her, or that Goneril and Regan have quite a good case against their father? Is there any real dramatic justification for the sub-plot? Does Lear really come to 'see the truth' during the storm and in his madness? If we look at what he says there with a properly critical eye, how can we accept it as marking a real spiritual progress in him? Again, why are the 'good' characters so often brought to affirm a clear moral pattern only for it to be subverted by the very next turn of events? Does any value at all in the play survive this sort of irony? If it is impossible to accept Lear's history as a spiritual progress, how can we avoid the conclusion that the play is utterly nihilistic, or alternatively, not a fully achieved success – that it is, as one critic has put it, 'radically incoherent'?

Questions like these are surely inescapable, and so is the critical conclusion to which they point – if, that is, we grant the basic assumption about the action of the drama. But I don't think we should grant it; nor do I find the play either nihilistic or incoherent. Its greatness seems to me more securely founded than that.[1]

[1] As there is little point in trying to note every agreement or disagreement with other critics of *King Lear*, I have kept such notes to a bare minimum. However, there are three recent and very pertinent discussions of the play I would like to mention here, since they came to my notice too late to use in developing my argument: Stanley Cavell, *Must We Mean What We Say?* (New York, 1969), pp. 267–353; A. L. French, *Shakespeare and the Critics* (Cambridge, 1972), ch. 4; and Marvin Rosenberg, *The Masks of King Lear* (Los Angeles, 1972).

　　With each of these I found a hearteningly large measure of agreement in our interpretations of the play, even though approaching it from different points of view and reaching different conclusions about it. Mr French, for example, also criticizes the common 'Bradleyan' interpretation; but he seems to accept an essentially 'Bradleyan' view of the action. Evidently he can see no positive alternative; and so, finding the play prompting questions it cannot answer, he concludes that it is only a dubious success. Mr Cavell's general view of it, on the other hand, is more positive; and in some respects my own view comes very close to his, even down to using some similar terms of analysis and argument. Mr Cavell's engagement with the text, however, seems rather too selective, so that his account of it, suggestive though it is, becomes somewhat limited and inconclusive. Nevertheless, like Mr French's, it is both stimulating and usefully provocative.

　　Mr Rosenberg stays close to the text all through; indeed, his book is perhaps the best detailed commentary on it available. He proceeds scene by scene, noting the wide range of theatrical interpretations each has received; and again and again I found my own sense of the text generally corroborating his. Where it did not, the difference usually arose from what seems to me a limitation in Mr Rosenberg's method. No doubt it is only the defect of its virtue, but in one respect I think his book stays rather *too* close to the text. So attentive is it to all the details of the play and to their various interpretations, that it leaves unclear exactly how much each matters in the total sum. The commentary is always perceptive; but in being a meticulous running commentary, it somehow loses (or dissipates) any sense of the fierce, urgent, accumulating pressure under which the details are not only informed but shaped: the pressure, I mean, that originates in the *poetic* substance of the drama, that continually enforces 'obedience' to the logic of the action, and whose end is our own final need (and incapacity) to 'speak what we feel'.

6

I

The opening terms

It is not hard to see why many people find *King Lear* so unbearable that they virtually reject it. Even Dr Johnson found he had to agree with most of his age in preferring Tate's version; and although the genius of the stage has still proved able to transform the play to suit the different sentimentalities of our own day – ethical, Christian, absurdist, 'revolutionary', or whatever – literary criticism has generally managed to relieve with 'interpretation' what the eighteenth century could only remove by surgery. Johnson at least faced the play honestly, and (as usual) he put his finger on the central difficulty it presents – the difficulty, that is, of accepting what it brings us eventually to feel. It fills the mind, he said, 'with a perpetual tumult of indignation, pity, and hope . . . So powerful is the current of the poet's imagination, that the mind, which once ventures within it, is hurried irresistibly along.' Where this current takes us – or ought to have taken us – is to 'this important moral, that villany is never at a stop, that crimes lead to crimes, and at last terminate in ruin'; and yet, he argued, in the process Shakespeare's imagination somehow overleaped one vital truth – a truth that is the foundation-stone of Johnson's objection: 'all reasonable beings naturally love justice'. Justice, he thought, is precisely what the play denies us, and his argument suggests that by doing this

7

the play denies the tumult of our feelings their natural resolution.[1]

It is characteristic of Johnson that he assumes our feelings work in an essentially passive way: they react to the given stimuli, as it were, rather than actively respond to and help shape the object. Nevertheless, his point is perfectly fair as far as it goes. Not merely have we wanted and hoped for justice throughout the play, but we have been subtly led to expect it. We witness acts that cry out for justice (and men crying out for it); we also witness the countervailing strength of goodness and love; and then, with a ruthlessness that seems gratuitous, Shakespeare suddenly subjects goodness and love not so much to human malignancy as to a malignancy or a moral indifference he evidently thinks inherent in the very nature of things. Cordelia's death shatters Lear, of course; but as Johnson saw, it also shatters the emergent pattern *we* have glimpsed, which gradually aroused and then seemed about to satisfy our desire for some vindicating design. And as Johnson quite fairly asked, why should Shakespeare do that? It is not for Johnson a question merely of realism: 'a play in which the wicked prosper, and the virtuous miscarry, may doubtless be good, because it is a just representation of the common events of human life'. Obviously, life is not calculable, nor is the kind of justice we look for – the manifestation of some significant order, some logic in events, which gains or even forces our deepest assent – the kind that anyone can find in the world merely by putting his head out of a window and glancing around. Johnson knew the vanity of human wishes, and realized often enough that 'celestial wisdom' may have to '*make* the happiness she does not find'. As he saw it, the effort to make moral sense of our experience is a necessary

[1] *Johnson on Shakespeare*, ed. Walter Raleigh (London, 1925), pp. 159–61.

part of a full humanity – an effort that should never capitulate either to the obstinate resistance of life or to its capacity to inflict gratuitous, savage counter-strokes. Behind his wish for a satisfying justice at the end of *Lear* probably lies the feeling that this is exactly what Shakespeare had done, and that it was a kind of weakness in him that he had. Merely to represent life may be only a way of giving in to it.

One reply to Johnson might well be that we want Shakespeare to show us the moral significance of the ending precisely because it *is* 'a just representation of the common events of human life'. If we were not convinced of that, we would not be so concerned to find some meaning in it; and it is no answer to the problem merely to remove it by substituting a different ending. But an age without so tense and unrelenting a will to dominate experience as Johnson's might also want to reply to him that there is a different but equal strength in the ability to yield to life – in a 'negative capability' of the spirit (the phrase actually comes from a letter in which Keats had been discussing *King Lear*): a positive power quite distinct from mere passivity or fatalistic resignation; and that in *Lear* Shakespeare is at least as much concerned with spiritual patience as with spiritual force. This was very much the direction taken by Bradley, for example, whose account of the play, confused as it is in some respects, is nowhere near as muddled or crudely sentimental as some of his twentieth-century followers'. Unlike them, he discovered no revelation of heavenly justice or harmony in the play, nor even the promise of any. Despite his talk about Lear's 'redemption', he sums up the final result as rather 'a consciousness of greatness in pain, and of solemnity in the mystery we cannot fathom'. Believing, as he put it in his first Lecture ('The Substance of Shakespearean Tragedy'), that all the terms of moral or poetic

9

'justice and merit or desert' are 'untrue to our [final] imaginative experience' of any of the tragedies, and that whatever emotions it involves 'the tragic position' does not involve judgment, he saw *King Lear* as held by the tension of two characteristic, opposing tendencies in Shakespeare. On the one hand was the tendency to regard worldly power and prosperity as merely the breeding-ground of hardness, vice, and destruction, and certainly not the gods' just reward for goodness – the tendency, indeed, to regard every outward circumstance, including misfortune and death, as the adversary *against* which the hero's soul is tested and improved, but as ultimately irrelevant to the reality of the soul and its virtues. Thus all 'error, guilt, failure, woe and waste' could come at times to seem finally unreal, 'illusive'. On the other hand, however, was the tendency to feel that 'suffering and death do matter greatly, and that happiness and life are not to be renounced as worthless', that some evil is equally real, and being real 'apparently cureless'. In answer to Swinburne's view of *Lear*, Bradley concluded that while Shakespeare does seem to have been so horrified at the power of evil that he was 'forced . . . sometimes to yield to the infirmity of misanthropy and despair' and to seek refuge in the thought of life as only a dream, nevertheless he also found in his art a way to help free himself of this perilous stuff, and to learn the 'patience' that this play, like *The Tempest*, 'seems to preach to us from end to end'.[1]

One obvious difficulty with this of course is what Bradley means by 'patience' (or what he thinks Shakespeare meant) – a question he does not press. The word can apply to very different states of mind, states that evade such broad, predetermined, and therefore unhelpful distinctions

[1] A. C. Bradley, *Shakespearean Tragedy*, 2nd ed. (London, 1952 [1905]), pp. 32–3, 278–9, 322ff.

as Stoic or Christian. It can mean, for example, a very rare, creative receptivity and wholeness (though such a state would hardly have much to do with preaching); or an almost irresponsible or virtually masochistic surrender of self; or again, as L. C. Knights has rightly observed of the 'patience' that *is* preached in Act IV of *Lear*, a condition hardly distinguishable from despair.[1] The reasons a man uses the word 'patience' may say far more about his state than the word itself. Nor does Bradley's account of the play quite face the question Johnson implicitly asks, which is not so much why (if at all) there is 'an element of reconciliation' in our feelings about the death of Cordelia, nor the rather more difficult question of why (if at all) we feel anything like this about the death of Lear, but rather why, despite Johnson, we can acknowledge these events as somehow a fitting close to the structure, the logic, of the play as a created whole. Bradley does speak of the final and total result as 'one in which pity and terror . . . are . . . blended with a sense of law and breauty';[2] and in that 'sense of law and beauty', which he obviously felt, lie the grounds of an answer to Johnson. But if Bradley was right in pointing to it, as I believe he was, his account of the play is not really a consistent attempt to explain it. In fact, the difficulty of explaining it seems to have drawn him at times (as it is likely to draw anyone) towards an idealistically over-simple view of what needs explaining.

II

That he never wholly succumbs to the temptation is a mark of Bradley's characteristic strength, and distinguishes his essays very sharply from what might be called the

[1] L. C. Knights, *Some Shakespearean Themes* (London, 1959), p. 106.
[2] Bradley, *Shakespearean Tragedy*, p. 279.

'Christianizing' interpretations that have proliferated since. Many of these could hardly be called particularly sensitive or even sensible, but generally speaking they view the play as a statement, or an illustration, or an allegory, or an affirmation, of a traditional Christian order. Most efforts to identify the pattern of the play with the pattern of Providence invite Gibbon's dry comment that the moral government of the Deity can be explained very readily merely by supposing the misfortunes of the wicked to be *judgments*, and those of the virtuous to be *trials*. We may not agree with Bradley that moral judgment has no place at all in our ultimate response to the tragedies, but his objections to supposing that it is to patterns of 'poetic justice' we are responding are still cogent. There is a far-reaching truth in his remark that 'we might not object to the statement that Lear deserved to suffer for his folly, selfishness and tyranny; but to assert that he deserved to suffer what he did suffer is to do violence not merely to language but to any healthy moral sense'.[1] Even at the best, there remains a discrepancy between reading the play and reading most 'Providential' accounts of it: the former leaves somewhat less obvious the moral justice of Gloucester's having his eyes torn out, for example, or the salvation of Lear's soul by means of his alleged 'self-knowledge', or the decisive redemptive power of Cordelia, or the ultimate insignificance of her death, or the happy release of Lear's soul. Whatever can be said about these aspects of the play, most people surely still feel the kind of doubts and hesitations Johnson and Bradley expressed; and not surprisingly a number of critics in recent years have been provoked to return to them.

These critics see the play's aesthetic order as affirming not a cosmic order, Christian or otherwise, but rather the

[1] *Ibid.*, p. 32.

absence of any. For some, the play is essentially nihilistic, or even destructively 'absurdist'; for others, it is a masterfully creative presentation of a 'world of extreme power and vitality embracing its opposite', which manages to make 'the unendurable endurable by bringing it within an artistic design, while retaining its essential truth' – to quote Barbara Everett's essay on 'The New *King Lear*'. For others again it evokes a morally ambiguous universe, which offers no providential support to human values but which does not invalidate them either. Most of these interpretations seem to me far more convincing (and humane) than those they are reacting against; certainly, I find myself agreeing with such critics at a great many points.[1] Nevertheless, if we do have to take the play's ironies and ending and creative power seriously, there still remains the question why we feel our own beings so profoundly involved – almost at stake – in its working out, and why its design evokes in us the 'sense of law' as well as the 'sense of beauty'. In as much as we do feel that, it suggests an attitude in Shakespeare rather more complex than Bradley himself described as a compound of horror, misanthropy, despair, and dualistic idealism – and certainly more troubled and questioning than anything that could simply be called 'Christian patience' or 'affirmation'. But it also seems in some ways finally more conclusive, more affirmative, than a merely 'artistic

[1] Barbara Everett, 'The New *King Lear*', *Critical Quarterly* (Winter, 1960), reprinted in Frank Kermode (ed.), *Shakespeare: King Lear*, Macmillan Casebook Series (London, 1969), pp. 184–202. Cf. William Empson's chapter, 'Fool in Lear', in *The Structure of Complex Words* (London, 1951), and his review of Maynard Mack's *King Lear in Our Time*, in *Essays in Criticism*, XVII (1967), 95–102; Nicholas Brooke, 'The Ending of *King Lear*', in Edward A. Bloom (ed.), *Shakespeare 1564–1964* (Providence, 1964), pp. 71–87; John D. Rosenberg, 'King Lear and His Comforters', *Essays in Criticism*, XVI (1966), 135–46; D. J. Enright, *Shakespeare and the Students* (London, 1970), ch. 1.

design' drawn upon a merely ambiguous universe would imply. Miss Everett is clearly right in saying that the play exhibits and enables in us a responsive awareness that 'can understand and endure imaginatively actions of great suffering, and by understanding can master them'; we do have the sense that we understand *something*. But that being so, perhaps the impulse to define that something in Christian terms is itself revealing, for the play surely leaves us with an attitude more active – steadier, more comprehensive, and freer – than (to take Bradley's description again, since it is not untypical) a mixture of pity and terror and an 'element of reconciliation' with the mystery we cannot fathom. The Christian interpretations do at least testify to a substantial logic in the action, a sense of law (which is not at all the same as a sense of resolution, of course, though the two are often confused): a feeling that the play does exhibit a 'justice' in things, in some significant, if not obvious, sense of the word. That it is not Christian Providence, I would agree: to see it as that one has finally to turn aside, with whatever degree of pain, from the full reality of the last scene. Nor can anyone do more than offer the most coherent account of it one can. But it may perhaps be that the last scene is so unbearable not because it denies us the justice we want, but because it gives it to us; and also perhaps that some of the mystery of which Bradley spoke, is to fathom *in ourselves* how much, as human beings, we can love justice if we are able to love at all.

III

Clearly, Johnson is right about all reasonable beings loving justice; but so too is Hamlet: 'use every man after his desert, and who should 'scape whipping?' Both observations are eminently reasonable – which is no doubt why so often we find it hard to *be* reasonable. When we want mercy or love, for example, we sometimes want them categorically, beyond any question of justice: we feel that they ought to be given freely even if they are not deserved, that perhaps in the last analysis they are 'superfluous' and no one actually deserves them. On the other hand, we sometimes feel that they ought to be given (especially to ourselves) just because they *are* deserved: it is only just. Again, if we love justice, we also love individual human beings; and Johnson's way of putting it usefully reminds us that we often find ourselves tugged less by our feelings on the one side and moral considerations on the other, than by conflicting feelings, each of which carries moral obligations with it. Then again, while we have to mete out justice and yet want the kind of love that is not amenable to measurement, we can readily turn about and say, if our own love for another seems to go beyond questions of measure, that it is only justice we want in wanting an equally unconstrained love in return. And it is here of course that human needs can become even more disastrously self-entangled. People can become so confused, so vulnerable, and so afraid of their vulnerability, that they hardly know what they want; and to add to the trouble, their desire for justice and their desire for love, even their need to love, can seem to betray weakness as much as exhibit strength, so that in the end they are hardly able to tell which is which.

It is naturally easier to see this sort of confusion in other people than to bear it in oneself; and as I think Johnson's argument half-suggests, it is from one to the other that the current of the poet's imagination hurries us – from the spectacle of Lear's tumult of feelings and the justice he wants, to the eventual tumult of our feelings and the justice we want. It does this, however, only because the process involves us right from the beginning much more actively, with more emotional and moral complicity, than Johnson allows. The very first scene, which determines so much for the rest of the play, leads us from a detached acceptance and expectancy to disappointment, dismay, indignation, and pity: to feelings and judgments actively aroused yet soon tangling themselves in a painful knot. For some people, Cordelia is wholly in the right; for others, she is not; for most, however, she is more in the right than Lear. But the scene does not offer us clear distinctions between right and wrong, good and bad, so much as draw us into sympathetic engagement with both characters even while we are beginning to fathom something deeply awry in each. We are even drawn to acknowledge the commonsense truth in Goneril's and Regan's final comments on the scene, though we are already chilled by their tone, the ease with which they drop their masks; they slip into prose as if it were their natural medium. Theirs is a kind of self-possession, a kind of measured detachment, we instinctively (and significantly) reject from the start.

The air of folk-tale ceremony makes this first scene curiously ambiguous, which is probably why our view of it – not just what moral judgments we make, but in what terms we grasp the characters, even what we conceive to be at issue – controls how we take the rest of the play. Explanations, causes, motives are apparently unnecessary at first – they are either simplified or just left out; later, however, when we are led to look back for them, it seems rather as if the characters may have been concealing them, even from themselves. An apparently firm, external, socially bonding order at once arouses and controls everyone's expectations (including ours); the emotions that suddenly flare out of it seem therefore especially naked and disruptive.

But as well as that, they also come to seem absolute, elemental, and to have been at work all the time beneath the surface. Nevertheless, it works the other way too. The folk-tale quality helps to determine our sense of human character, not only heightening but also delimiting the ways in which these characters exist *as* human characters for us. Especially in its contrast with the easy, everyday, conversational tone of the opening between Kent, Gloucester and Edmund, the tone and movement of the ceremony and its subsequent breakdown create the 'characters' in it in specific, though not easily describable, terms. We have to grasp them not primarily as ethical agents, deciding what to do in a carefully defined context of choices, far less as individuals with a particular history, idiosyncratic traits of behaviour, and a private, complex personality. They emerge here more in terms of particular, individual ways of *feeling* – feeling the affections and obligations that constitute such basic self-identifying relationships as kingship, fatherhood, daughterhood, service, and so on – but ultimately, I think in terms of different ways of responding to the very capacity to feel at all. Hence their rather archetypal quality, for whatever ethical or psychological density they gain later on relates to this basic human capacity.

Part of the tremendously swift and powerful action of the scene is to make us apprehend the characters in just this way. Lear's opening speech appears at first a perfectly natural beginning to a ceremony, even if rather a strange one. Regal, formal, authoritative, he simply wills the division of the kingdom, and prepares to bestow its riches upon his children. If this already disturbs us a little as a potentially dangerous act, it is after all the natural office of a king to will and of a parent to bestow. No resistant fact comes between self, authority, power, and deed; in truth,

I doubt if anyone immersed in the immediate event expects any as yet, no matter what the Elizabethan World-Picture says about politics, families, or the behaviour proper to old men. In any case, Lear's reference to a 'darker intent' seems only to remind us that kings have their own good reasons for what they do – though it does evoke, very briefly, the hint of a mystery behind what we see. When he talks of 'crawling towards death', the rhythms and tone hardly seem those of a man with his mind on Last Things: the phrase sounds rather too much like a mere rhetorical gesture, or at most an item of business merely to be noted here and dealt with later. At this stage we are far from asking the sort of question George Orwell raised, for instance – whether Lear is really renouncing the world or being self-indulgently irresponsible (though that particular way of putting the alternatives begs some important questions).[1] Nor do we yet ask ourselves how far Lear's own question – 'Which of you shall we say doth love us most?' – is only a gesture, since the kingdom is already apportioned and the real decisions already taken, and how far it is a sign of some need in him so voracious that it could never be wholly satisfied. So far, we are hardly aware of him in a way that prompts this kind of question. Nor, for that matter, is there anyone who does not expect it will be the third daughter who loves him most. Not merely do all the characters obviously expect it, but the whole sequence makes us assume it too. What Cordelia does, however, initiates a pattern that recurs throughout the whole play: reality shatters what the mind and feelings expect of it. For by bringing the sequence to an abrupt halt, disrupting the social and emotional order implicit in it, which no one has questioned, by insisting on a

[1] George Orwell, 'Lear, Tolstoy and the Fool', in Kermode (ed.), *Shakespeare: King Lear*, pp. 150–68.

real identity on quite other terms, and by refusing to compromise her judgment and will – her individual freedom – in the slightest, Cordelia does more than make that order now seem a nasty form of constraint. By evoking another view of it, and wholly committing herself to that view, she also forces individual reality on the other characters as well – and, in another way, on us. They now have to act out of what they really are, rather than play the role Lear's ceremony had given them; we have to understand (which of course involves us in judging) for ourselves what they really are; and the reality put before us, and in terms of which we naturally respond, is their openness to and capacity for honest feeling and what then goes with that: the importance they attach to this capacity in themselves and in others. To be sure, the way things happen hardly allows anyone to pause and consider them until later, in retrospect, when the implications have become starkly plain. As Johnson pointed out, the whole play is like that, and it is important not to distort our account of it by ignoring the fact. Even Cordelia's asides, though they make us suspicious of her sisters' sincerity, hardly make us realize at this stage how much of themselves Goneril and Regan betray in their answers to Lear – the desire for possession in the one, and the coiling self-regard in the other – or that Lear has given them substitutes for love rather than tokens of it. It is not long before it does become clear that the two sisters' real nature was not obscured but actually revealed by the merely formal roles they had seemed only to be playing, and that so was part of Lear's real nature too. But once Cordelia refuses to play a role at all, the current sweeps everyone out among the immediate, but still half-submerged dangers of real emotions.

Cordelia is obviously trapped in a dilemma – one not

unlike Hamlet's, but one that also arises again and again for other characters in the course of this play. For how can she act so that what she is – her full being – is both contained and expressed fully, freely, without loss or exaggeration, in what she does and says? If she chooses 'to love and be silent', that would make her seem less than she is. Merely to utter the word, 'nothing', is inadequate too: as Gloucester remarks on another, related occasion, 'the quality of nothing hath not such need to hide itself' (I, ii, 33), and she is conscious of feeling too much for 'nothing' to *mean* nothing. In rejecting the ceremony and any role in it as a mere fiction, she is equally impelled by a bitter hostility to the 'glib and oily art' of her sisters which Lear has encouraged; and being full of that, she has to speak, and speak 'truth'. In ways more basic than we realize as yet, she is a true daughter of the man who thinks he could measure out love its just deserts, and who, when he is himself trapped later on, can deceive himself into thinking he could be 'the pattern of all patience; I will say nothing' but who is far too passionately alive to do or be anything of the kind, and whose own obstinate strength is never to abate his demands on life. So she naturally proceeds to measure out her love for him with the most absolute justice: 'according to my bond; no more or less'. She speaks 'truth' for the sake of being 'true'. Nevertheless, in refusing to have any truck with fiction or a social role based upon it, and acting partly out of an unacknowledged weakness in herself – that is, out of a need to feel and to appear more righteous than her sisters – she succeeds in turning her 'truth' into falsehood.

It is equally easy to over-value and to under-value Cordelia's action here. Since her identity includes her own consciousness of herself – a self-image, as it were, necessarily inadequate to the reality, but nevertheless necessary to define and regulate it – the need to commit herself in action while yet preserving the only sense of herself she can respect (a problem faced by many of Shakespeare's tragic figures, of course) inevitably makes her dilemma a cruel one. For both she and Lear seem to realize as well as anyone what is at stake – a gesture, even a conventional one, to acknowledge the reality of love – only neither of them can admit it. Reasonably enough, he has assumed (so that we do too, I think) that she really knows or can see what he feels for her, and that he knows what she really feels for him:

> Now, our joy,
> Although our last, and least; to whose young love
> The vines of France and milk of Burgundy
> Strive to be interess'd; what can you say to draw
> A third more opulent than your sisters? Speak.[1] (I, i, 82ff)

The warmth and natural richness of this, and the blatant if self-advertising generosity in it ('a third *more* opulent'), declare his feelings and assumptions pretty unmistakably. But the speech she feels she has to make does not show much basis for them: first 'Nothing, my lord'; then 'According to my bond; no more nor less'; and eventually;

> Good my Lord,
> You have begot me, bred me, lov'd me: I
> Return those duties back as are right fit,
> Obey you, love you, and most honour you.
> Why have my sisters husbands, if they say
> They love you all? Happily, when I shall wed,
> That lord whose hand must take my plight shall carry
> Half my love with him, half my care and duty:
> Sure I shall never marry like my sisters,
> To love my father all.

It is impossible not to sympathize with her: what else

---

[1] All quotations are from the New Arden edition of *King Lear*, edited by Kenneth Muir, London, 1964.

could one say in public circumstances like these that would not either be or sound false? A possible theme might have been something easier and lighter, like 'There's beggary in the love that can be reckoned'; but of course only someone more self-assured, less defensive, than Cordelia could have seen that or said it. What she does say is perfectly fair – in a way. Taken in themselves, or in another context, or in another tone even, her words would be wholly 'true', as Lear himself seems almost to recognize; his reply suggests that he thinks her perhaps the dutifully spoken daughter who has simply mistaken the occasion. But as many critics have noted, there are two important things badly awry in her speech, even though she cannot be simply blamed for them. Because there is so much about her sisters in it, it says far more clearly what she feels for them than what she feels for her father: at bottom, it is almost addressed more to them than to him. More importantly, however, the only way she can find to assert the integrity and freedom she rightly claims is by seeing nature and natural duty as constraining her very capacity to love, just as, she assumes, they have constrained his. She denies both the freely given (indeed, ostentatiously generous) current of his love and the very 'I' she speaks of. Seeing nature only as a system of external bonds, she denies the freedom, the activity, the responsibility, the spontaneity of *both* selves. As the author of *The Merchant of Venice* clearly realized, if all natural relationships do depend on 'bonds', human relationships – and especially the love of one human being for another – are not natural bonds in the limited sense Cordelia is giving the word here. Conceived so defensively, issuing from too tightly guarded a consciousness of oneself, the meaning of the word inevitably starts to drift towards the merely external – towards Shylock's sense, as it were; and conceived in that way, a 'bond' can ultimately yield no more than a justice correspondingly constricted, 'heartless', and therefore self-defeating. For all Cordelia's distance from Shylock, her language does subtly negate Lear's identity: not just by denying his emotional freedom, but even more by ignoring altogether the unutterable plea for reassurance that prompts such questions as his, however ridiculous or embarrassing or improper they are. Consequently, his reply to her speech is doubly to the point – indeed it is the crucial test of her truth:

> But goes thy heart with this?

The moment of silence before he asks that question is where we begin to feel for him; her answer – 'Ay, my good Lord' – is where we may well begin to judge her. If there was still a degree of obstinate integrity in her earlier 'Nothing', this – in the light of what she must know he wants, and in the light of the unyielding self-righteousness in the rhythms and syntax of her speech – is little more than an obstinate untruth. There is too much conscious rectitude, too much merely reactive ego, in her speech, too little actively ventured and given, for real integrity now. Her 'heart' is precisely what it leaves out. Clearly there is something wrong with a man who requires love to display itself on demand; on the other side, however, there is also something wrong with a heart that answers only to the demand rather than to the need (or the love) behind it.

For need it is; and I think Coleridge was essentially right in his account of it. He notes in Cordelia 'something of disgust at the ruthless hypocrisy of her sisters, some little faulty admixture of pride and sulleness'; and in Lear a

strange yet by no means unnatural, mixture of selfishness, sensibility, and habit of feeling derived from and fostered by the particular rank and usages of the individual; the intense desire to be intensely beloved, selfish, and yet characteristic of the selfishness of a loving and kindly nature – a feeble selfishness, self-supportless and leaning for all pleasure on another's breast; the selfish craving after a sympathy with a prodigal disinterestedness, contradicted by its own ostentation and the mode and nature of its claims; . . . anxiety, . . . distrust, . . . jealousy . . .[1]

Lear's outburst, 'Let it be so . . .', reveals more than mere rage, however – at least to us, if not to himself. This speech is like an answering correlative to Cordelia's. Against the self-restricting rhythm of hers, her consciousness aggressively intent on measuring herself out 'no more nor less', his is equally tightly checked at first, though to a different end: his consciousness is intent on holding emotion back until it has collected all of its aggressive power. He invokes nature as distant, sacred, and mysterious – the sun, Hecate, night, 'the operation of the orbs' – as against the human operations of 'begot . . . bred . . . lov'd' in her speech, but his inner eye is paying no more attention to what he evokes than hers did. What she could see was what her state of mind needed to see: only a pattern of obligation laid upon her, as though she had no will to love of her own. His state turns to the other side of it: vast and irresistible powers are summoned to sanction a climactic act of will, an act that, in separating his self from his 'heart', is equally false to his feelings and his integrity:

> Here I disclaim all my paternal care,
> Propinquity and property of blood,
> And as a stranger to my heart and me
> Hold thee from this for ever.

Both of them see nature simply as external to their inmost

[1] Coleridge, *Shakespearean Criticism*, ed. Thomas Middleton Raysor, 2 vols. (Everyman's Library, London, 1960). I, 54, 49–50.

selves: she, as if it imposed 'bonds' on her; he, as if its bonds could be disclaimed by a mere act of will.

But Lear seems forced to go beyond the stop after 'forever', driven on by a still unappeased, hidden frustration:

> The barbarous Scythian,
> Or he that makes his generation messes
> To gorge his appetite, shall to my bosom
> Be as well neighbor'd, pitied, and reliev'd,
> As thou my sometime daughter.

Of course it is Lear doing most of the gorging here – the dramatic irony, the self-deception, is too sharp to miss. But what drives him to project in this way, and in fantasies so violently disproportionate to the occasion, is surely what leads him to the image, in the midst of these horrors, of a comforting bosom. (After all, why should he imagine a barbarian capable of such things ever *needing* pity and relief?) He seems impelled less by any thought of Cordelia's possible distress in the future than by a desire he cannot admit even to his own consciousness – to be himself neighboured, pitied, and relieved in her bosom ('thou mads't thy daughters thy mothers'). His next words, to Kent, make the point almost explicit:

> Come not between the Dragon and his wrath.
> I lov'd her most, and thought to set my rest
> On her kind nursery. Hence, and avoid my sight!

He can admit his wish for rest and comfort, to be satisfied on his own terms; what he cannot acknowledge, although his speech and actions exhibit it to us, is his need of them. Nor can he acknowledge what we discern ultimately lies behind that, his need to love, since Cordelia will not allow his love except on her terms.

For if the terms of his demand prevent the flow of Cordelia's love, it is equally true (as Arthur Sewell has noted, for example)[1] that the terms of her reply do the same to him. Whatever Lear had said himself, and whatever is said by critics seeking profound moral faults in his behaviour to explain why his later suffering is so providentially just, his division of the kingdom had not been attempting to calculate the worth of his daughters' love against material possessions, or *vice versa*. The division being already settled, he was surreptitiously asking them, and especially Cordelia, rather to measure *his* love by the generosity of his gift. Whatever his reasons for abdicating (and the very perfunctoriness with which they are mentioned is significant), he clearly saw himself as a good and just father bestowing notably splendid estates on his children, and the declaration he wanted from each of them was surely the acknowledgment of his own paternal and regal largeness of heart. That he gave Goneril and Regan their share without much evident affection to go with it does not make his action despicable (at least he has given them justice if not love); but it is precisely because he *was* giving Cordelia love with his gift that her response has hurt so badly. She has seemed to deny not so much the gift as the love, and she has done so, moreover, in a way that denies *him* by denying his ability to respect himself as a man of careful justice, noble generosity, and love for (especially one of) his children. It is only later, when she can respond with the love and respect Lear needs, that he can cease to feel his very identity at stake in getting them, and so cease to demand them. Just so, it is only when his conscious sense of his own identity collapses, and he therefore no longer confuses the kind of love

<hr/>

[1] Arthur Sewell, *Character and Society in Shakespeare* (Oxford, 1951), pp. 60ff, 112, 115.

and respect he wants with the kind his self really needs, that she can freely give them.

In this first scene, however, he is denied rest and comfort where he had been most confident of getting them; more basically indeed, denied the kind of satisfaction he had wanted for his own need of loving, active and passive. The kind of love he wants would at once endorse the only image of himself he can respect and therefore acknowledge, remain silent about the need, and thereby enable him not to be conscious of the terrifying vulnerability from which it springs. The psychological shock of being denied it is so great that he can only turn himself into a Dragon, which cannot feel love and therefore does not need 'relief'. He wraps himself in ethical rights, in punitive authority, in images of invulnerable and implacable power: 'the bow is bent and drawn; make from the shaft'; 'to come betwixt our sentence and our power, . . . nor our nature nor our place can bear'; and so on. He seizes on any external strength with which he can readily identify, and so protect, the self – though his real need, born out of an unacknowledged helplessness, is for a very different kind of satisfaction. The inevitable result, of course, is an appalling violence and injustice.

The spectacle Cordelia offers in this first scene, then, is something less than one of wronged virtue, and Lear something more than one of blind folly and self-will. (That is only the sort of moralistically simple view of it that Goneril and Regan take at the end of it.) The king of France's remark is clearly relevant to both father and daughter. In different but related ways, both of them mingle love with 'regards that stand/ Aloof from th'entire point', helplessly tainting it with something else. The very simplicity and dignity with which France himself can pass by such regards only underlines the obvious fact that Lear and Cordelia are too open to hurt from each other to want less than too much: each of them demands the 'justice' necessary to the person it most pleases each to be, and so aborts his own feelings by refusing to let the other love in the only way he can at this point. In fact, neither really attends to the full reality of the other at all, since neither, it seems, can admit the whole of his own being into his consciousness. Each becomes locked in his self-conscious ego, and one driven ego becomes locked hard against the other: one imperfect consciousness against the other, one tightly knotted will against the other . . . Two wrongs don't make a right, but people who are close are often willing to take them as a very acceptable substitute.

IV

One reason why the next meeting of these particular 'hard hearts' – the reconciliation scene at the end of Act IV – is so moving is that each does simply yield, not only to the other but also to itself, both of them at last releasing what has been visible to us all along. The reversals from the opening obviously comment on both scenes. A little before they meet we have already seen Cordelia evoking a very different sense of nature – sustaining corn, idle weeds, blessed secrets, all the 'unpublish'd virtues of the earth' – its healing powers clearly the external correlative of her own power to weep (IV, iv). As she bends over her sleeping father, pity and love now do 'place thy medicine on my lips'. It is now she who imagines neighbouring, pitying, and relieving:

> Mine enemy's dog,
> Though he had bit me, should have stood that night
> Against my fire . . .   (IV, vii, 36–8)

and she is thinking of Lear, not of herself. And it is now she who invokes the gods, in words that might – and perhaps should – have been said in the first scene, when Lear was 'child-changed' enough in another sense, if only she had been able not to abuse her own nature and say them:

> O you kind Gods,
> Cure this great breach in his abused nature!
> Th'untuned and jarring senses, O! wind up
> Of this child-changed father.   (*ibid.*, 14–17)

For Lear, on the other hand, it now appears that *he* is bound

> Upon a wheel of fire, that mine tears
> Do scald like molten lead . . .

But these bonds are not dissociated from the self, not thought of as external, constraining objects. Rather, they define the very shape and substance of his present self. Moreover, since he is now in his more 'perfect mind', he can admit his fear that he is not. Probably the most poignant moment in the whole scene is that where each self, free now of all role-playing, at last acknowledges with naked simplicity both its own reality and that of the other.

> LEAR I am a very foolish fond old man . . .
> Do not laugh at me;
> For as I am a man, I think this lady
> To be my child Cordelia.
> COR.   And so I am, I am. (*ibid.*, 60ff)

This is more than 'self-knowledge' in Lear – a recovery of true sight which 'redeems' him from his earlier blind folly and self-ignorance. The point is not what he now knows, but what he now is; and it is a point vital to our understanding of the whole play. Lear can know what he knows here, and know it in the manner he does, only because of more far-reaching changes in his very self. The fear that lay behind his rage is dissolved in being able to acknowledge his helplessness, or at least in not being able to deny it. His conscious will is now dissolved in another kind of will altogether, one not separate from the capacity to be acted upon, the capacity to feel and to suffer without trying to deny that he does so, although it is worth noticing that his will is even now not wholly purified: the pain of conscious guilt bends him towards self-destruction before Cordelia assuages the guilt, as later on the delight of consciously loving and being loved will bend it towards a kind of indulgent evasiveness. But here his 'authority' is no longer what it was before – a conscious possession, an instrument, a quality he could regard as objectively his and upon which he could base his own self-respect. Here he is unconscious of authority altogether, not because his idea of it earlier was a delusion, but because 'authority' now means something quite different – it is a quality that we, like Cordelia, can acknowledge (where he cannot) because it is now the outward mark not of his conscious self-image, but of his actual being, of what he is. Able now to acknowledge his feelings of guilt and shame, he is able to acknowledge his feelings of love and need too. In doing that, he can accept more of himself into his conception of himself; but it is the ability to do so, not the conception, that really matters. It is because he can be so much more in possession of himself that he can likewise respect himself in a quite different sense, and in doing that also acknowledge the independent reality of Cordelia's selfhood – the independence his fear could not initially allow him to acknowledge as real, even though it was the only possible condition of what he really wanted. In short, just as father and daughter each acknowledges an ultimate dependence on, and vulnerability to, the other as the very 'heart' of his own identity, so each fact they acknowledge depends on all the others, each being both a condition and a consequence of the rest.

Thus Cordelia's 'truth' – her own reality, her sense of reality, her genuine rectitude, even her will – now can be expressed too, but only by a kind of falsehood, a fiction or 'lie' that speaks precisely the part of the truth she had denied:

> LEAR . . . If you have poison for me, I will drink it.
> I know you do not love me; for your sisters
> Have, as I do remember, done me wrong:
> You have some cause, they have not.
> COR.   No cause, no cause.   (*ibid.*, 72–5)

In the face of what he feels, how else could love declare itself except by that denial? The relevant truth does not consist merely in being true to one's conscious sense of oneself, nor merely in uttering words justly apportioned to facts and rights and duties as though these were entirely external to oneself. Since it also requires the more difficult act of expressing in the public world one's innermost being – a self that can sustain its integrity only by keeping the 'heart' perilously open – it has to risk the dangers of fiction.

Shakespeare had already looked at the implications of that in *Hamlet*, of course, and he was to look again in *Antony and Cleopatra*. For the danger is not just what Cordelia, like Hamlet, at first supposed – that others may utter forgeries of the real thing. However deeply moving and necessary is the truth of Cordelia's 'no cause, no cause' (and it is the only apology she makes), this is still not the whole of the truth either.[1] What happened in the first scene and has happened since is (like Dolabella's Antony as distinct from

---

[1] One of the few critics to notice this is Nicholas Brooke, 'The Ending of *King Lear*', in Bloom (ed.), *Shakespeare 1564–1964*, p. 81.

Cleopatra's 'Emperor') also real. Lear has something to feel guilty about, and even here his feelings still tend irresistibly towards himself: 'I am mightily abus'd. I should e'en die with pity/To see another thus.' Nor, for that matter, is he wholly a 'poor *perdu*', a victim, as Cordelia supposes. His face was not just 'oppos'd against the warring winds', it was urging them on. In short, to see him as Cordelia does, as deserving only pity, is to do less than justice to his all-too-human humanity. And that, surely, is why the play cannot finish at the end of Act IV, despite the tendency of many critics to talk rather as if it did. For reasons significantly akin to those that apply to Acts IV and V of *Antony and Cleopatra*, it has not yet done justice to what it has evoked for *us*. The 'great rage' is killed in Lear (not by 'self-knowledge', incidentally, but by sleep naturally supervening on sheer exhaustion), yet as it is killed so some part of him seems to go with it. The inner release and self-possession of the reconciliation scene are not the release and possession of his whole self. After all, which seems to us the more fully alive as a human being, the man who can only beg humbly and frankly,

> . . . You must bear with me.
> Pray you now, forget and forgive: I am old and foolish,

or the man whose characteristic energy flashes out later: 'I killed the slave that was a-hanging thee'? Not one more than the other, surely; and yet that answer only raises another question. When we recall what we have seen him and others (especially others) actually do, does 'forget and forgive' really seem to us enough, just like that? Given everything we are conscious of, including Lear's own suffering and his pitiful diminishment by it, do we not also (as reasonable beings) still want 'the powers of the kingdom' to come to 'an arbitrement'? Which of us thinks at the time that 'forget and forgive' was appropriate for Cornwall's blinding of Gloucester or for Cordelia's hangman?

It is no wonder that many people see the play as finally only a terrible, even unbearable, negation. It is harder to see why it seems to others to exhibit some law, though not a specifically Christian one, and to achieve, perhaps thereby, a beauty that is not merely aesthetic. Nevertheless, whether he can answer it or not, this does seem the central question any critic of the play has to try to meet, and meet moreover from within the terms offered by the play itself.

2

Sight, 'vision', and action

The reconciliation scene, I have suggested, shows in Lear more than a recognition of the facts, a recovery of 'sight' from his earlier 'blindness'. Although it is often put in some such way, the point of the scene is not so much what Lear now comes to *see*, as what he can now *acknowledge* – less, that is, a matter of facts which were there all along and which he at last perceives, than of his being able at last to accept certain things, even if tacitly, *as* facts. Whether or not he also accepts them as good or bad is not the immediate question; the crucial thing here is that he accepts them as *real*. Only in so far as he does that – and it is only painfully and still only partially that he can – does he release their force, their significance, in himself and in Cordelia, and thus into the world as they apprehend it, and through that, into the world both of them evoke and embody to us.

To take one obvious example, they do not merely 'recognize' or 'see' the bond between them as though they had not seen it before. They were both very much aware of it earlier; but each of them, constraining his self, could acknowledge the bond he saw only as a constraint. Now, each of them, being able to face the vulnerability of his 'heart', not only enables himself *and* the other to love freely, but at the same time is able to acknowledge the fact that the other does so. What they can admit in themselves, painful as it is to admit it, they can allow to exist as a perceptible, objective reality. In short, the kind of bond they 'see' is the kind of bond they can realize in themselves. Here, just as in the first scene, it answers exactly to how each of them conceives his own identity and thus how much of themselves goes into acknowledging the existence of the bond. The 'facts' of it now are not the 'facts' of it then; the difference marks the difference between their earlier and later conceptions of themselves, and that in turn marks the differences in them both as people. Similarly, we could put it that Lear now 'sees' or 'recognizes' Cordelia as his true daughter, but the same applies once more. Since of course he, like everyone else, always knew she was that – the 'fact' being indeed the main ground of their obstinate demands on one another – putting it in this way tends to blunt the vital point of the drama, which is not to show him overlooking 'facts' and the moral implication of 'facts' there is never any question about and which he has only to have his eyes opened to 'see', but to make us question how the facts come to *be* facts: to question, that is, what Lear and Cordelia could acknowledge the relationship to consist in earlier and what they can now; and why; and whether her being a true daughter and his ability to acknowledge it do not, in the end, depend on each other.

Although this may seem mere quibbling over the word 'see', I think it goes further than that – especially since the metaphor of 'sight' is so thoroughly exploited by the play itself. When we ordinarily talk of 'seeing' we mean seeing an object, whether physical or mental: something we (quite properly) assume to exist before it is seen, which can be inspected and vouched for by others independently, and which can be adequately grasped or described in other terms than those of one particular view of it. To 'acknowledge' something, however, includes rather more: not merely a perception, but at the same time a decision of the mind, an ability, indeed a willingness – which involves more than the intellect, of course – to assent to its reality. To 'see' a truth, for instance, is really to acknowledge it as a truth. It only exists as an object to be 'seen' inasmuch as it is *accepted* as true.

That an act of judgment is involved in all our insights, and that all kinds of values subtly shape and direct the act, may be obvious enough; but applied to a play such as *King Lear* the point has implications not merely for how we find meaning in the work, but also for the kind of meaning we may expect to find. For once we start talking of what the characters 'see' – whether things or insights – we may quite unwittingly import the commonsense, 'realistic' assumptions implicit in the ordinary notion of seeing, when they can apply neither to the characters nor to Shakespeare.

I

The reasons why such realistic assumptions cannot apply have been presented a number of times and in a number of ways during the long controversy about 'character' in Shakespeare and 'Bradleyism' generally.[1] There is no need to disturb the controversial dust again, but a few things have become clearer than they once were. One is the very simple truth expressed in Johnson's remark, that 'nothing can please many, and please long, but just *representations* of general nature', and in Bradley's, that 'the essence of drama – and certainly of Shakespearean drama – lies in actions and

[1] The Bradleyan controversy has been very fully chronicled by Katherine Cooke, *A. C. Bradley and his Influence in Twentieth-Century Shakespeare Criticism* (Oxford, 1972). The application of such assumptions specifically to *King Lear* has been sharply questioned by Paul J. Alpers in his essay on 'King Lear and the Theory of the "Sight Pattern"', in Reuben A. Brower and Richard Poirier (eds.), *In Defense of Reading* (New York, 1962); see esp. pp. 134, 143.

words expressive of inward movements of human nature'.[1]
If characters are conventions abstracted by the reader from
his total response to the words of the play (a point that
Bradley himself insisted on, incidentally[2]), it is equally true
that the poetic medium of a Shakespearean tragedy reaches
us only as what one character or another says – a conventional condition that controls our response to the poetry at
every point. As for the inner 'character' given to each
dramatic figure by the play – his particular psychological
shape, his specific substance *as* an individual – Coleridge was
surely right. We infer it from what the figure says and does,
in the same manner as we infer the 'character' of people in
real life from what they say and do. Within the *données* and
the stylistic mode of the work, we naturally assume the
characters to be separate, autonomous centres of consciousness, with an inner life like that of real people – feelings,
thoughts, motives, desires, will, a capacity for growth and
change, idiosyncrasises, contradictions, and so on – in so
far as their words and actions evoke it. True, any dramatic
figure is a fiction created by means of artistic conventions,
and since conventions impose controls and limits on what
we can infer about the figure, the particular conventions of
a play ought to control the kind of information, and the
extent of it, we need to infer – even though (it is worth
adding) we cannot comprehend the particular conventions
of a play without the fullest imaginative response to it as
itself a unique whole. But if we can now agree that Shakespeare's tragedies are not more or less idealized documen-
taries, we do not have to conclude that they are therefore
visionary poems or abstract allegories instead. Given the

[1] *Johnson on Shakespeare*, ed. Raleigh, p. 11; A. C. Bradley, *Oxford Lectures on Poetry* (London 1917 [1909]), p. 388.
[2] *Oxford Lectures*, pp. 15–17.

dramatic and stylistic conventions, we inevitably seek some kind of coherent individuality and some significant likeness to our own life in the speeches and acts of a dramatic figure, and our searching for these things throughout the whole play is the main way by which the full meaning of the words is at once realized and controlled. As with the dramatic 'action', so with dramatic 'character'. Neither can be divorced from the poetry, nor it from them: to understand one is to understand the others. In fact, each is a medium in which the others are realized.

Looking back at the attack on Bradleyan character-study, I think we can detect another kind of reason for it. This appears in G. Wilson Knight's claim, for example, that interpretation of Shakespeare 'must be metaphysical rather than ethical', and that we should therefore concentrate on the 'visionary whole', the 'burning central core' of each play, which is conveyed by 'atmospheric suggestion' and 'direct poetic-symbolism' as much as by 'personification'.[1] Behind the various theoretical attacks on Bradley's alleged 'realism', I suspect, lay a similar unease about the particular ethical qualities in which Bradley supposed the reality of all human character to consist, and about the decisive importance he therefore seemed to give to these moral characteristics in Shakespearean tragedy. For even when Bradley turned to the metaphysical implication of the tragedies, to the world of good and evil which takes us (he argued) beyond the moral terms of justice and merit or desert, his terms do still seem rather constricting in being so ethically limited:

if we confine our attention to the hero, and to those cases where the gross and palpable evil is not in him but elsewhere, we find that the

---

[1] G. Wilson Knight, *The Wheel of Fire* (Oxford, 1930; rev. ed. London, 1949; corr. rev. ed. 1954 etc.; Methuen University Paperback ed., London, 1960), pp. 10–11.

comparatively innocent hero still shows some marked imperfection or defect, – irresolution, precipitancy, pride, credulousness, excessive simplicity, excessive susceptibility to sexual emotions, and the like. These defects or imperfections are certainly, in the wide sense of the word, evil, and they contribute decisively to the conflict and catastrophe.[1]

If it was this kind of thing that really made critics uneasy, it may help to explain the curiously persistent notion that *Shakespearean Tragedy* dates from the nineteenth century and treats Shakespeare's tragedies as psychological novels. It would be nearer the mark to say that Bradley approached Shakespeare with the firm ethical outlook, and the corresponding sense of character, that dominated the Victorian novel. The relevant objection to Bradley's approach, I think, is not that he thought of the plays as novels (for he didn't), even that he discussed 'character' when he should have discussed the poetry and the 'metaphysical' themes, but rather that, inasmuch as 'character' in the fullest sense is of decisive importance in human life and character-study can therefore help us understand Shakespeare's handling of life, Bradley's sense of what character actually consists in itself was inadequate – inadequate (as we now see) to the deeper, more intangible reaches of personal experience and personal identity in Shakespeare's tragedies as in real life. To put it another way: if behind Bradley there lay the achievement of the major Victorian novelists, with their stress on the determining force of specific moral characteristics, the achievement of the major novelists of the twentieth century as well as of the major poets – of Joyce and Lawrence, for example, as well as Yeats and Eliot (to mention only those writing in English) – with their more open, troubled, and problematic sense of human identity, was bound to make

[1] Bradley, *Shakespearean Tragedy*, pp. 34–5.

Bradley's seem too assured in some respects and too limited or vague in others. But because this kind of unease with Bradleyan character-study was never conclusively defined, it became confused with other things – ascribing to Shakespeare some brand or other of 'traditional' belief, for instance; or the theoretical status of 'character' as against 'plot' or dramatic conventions or 'direct poetic-symbolism'; or the supposed gap between the 'metaphysical' and the merely 'moral' in Shakespeare. This is probably why we find all too many critics, ostentatiously freeing us from the shackles of Bradleyism by insisting on the decisive dramatic importance of 'traditions' or 'conventions' or 'direct poetic-symbolism', in actual practice treating 'character', in so far as they do treat it, in very much the same terms as Bradley himself or in terms even more rigidly moralistic.

Clearly, what was needed was a conception of 'character' more adequate to reality as we know it, and hence to Shakespearean tragedy as we apprehend it – one that would do justice not only to our sense of the characters' moral autonomy in a world of good and evil (as Bradley's did), but also to the subtle, manifold ways in which the poetic medium and the controlling conventions work in each play so as simultaneously to create an appropriate kind of identity for the characters, give them a larger symbolic force, and comment on them. This could hardly be achieved by treating 'character' as a mere epiphenomenon, however. Shakespeare's characters (like any great dramatist's) are symbolic, as Wilson Knight insisted; but that does not make them mere symbols. Since the characters' experience must, in essentials at least, seem humanly real, it must seem to be really theirs, not just a put-up job by the author. This is not to deny that dramatic figures can be symbolic in many different ways, but it does mean that whatever else they are made to symbolize, they symbolize primarily the kind of experience, attitudes, and values that the whole play makes us see embodied in their consciousness, actions, sufferings, inter-relationships, and conflicts. Any interpretation of the play necessarily entails an interpretation of the characters, and *vice versa*; the critic can neither dismiss character as unimportant nor assume that Bradley has dealt with that aspect of the play so thoroughly that he himself can ignore it. On the contrary, he has to ask what the poetry and the total action actually realize *as* character – the precise terms in which it is made real for us and made to matter in the total effect. He requires, that is to say, a conception of character as more than a set of readily nameable moral qualities which motivate an individual's choices and actions in a supposedly pre-existing world. To respond to the poetry fully is to find it expressive of 'character' at a far more fundamental level, a level at which we might more accurately speak of 'identity' rather than 'character' or even 'personality'. For it consists in a particular, individual way of experiencing, indeed of actually apprehending, reality – or rather, since that may sound too passive, in a particular way of being humanly alive in *and to* the world. In the active manifestation of that life, both the individual's world and his individual self assume a specific reality and a morally significant shape.

To 'character' conceived in this way, the realistic assumptions implicit in the ordinary notion of 'seeing' cannot apply. Nor, for that matter, can they apply to Shakespeare either; and the reason (which Bradley himself understood)[1] is basically the same in both cases. With the characters, their words and actions are not merely contingent, dispensable devices by which they try to communicate their

[1] Bradley, *Oxford Lectures*, pp. 15-17.

thoughts or insights. They have no inner substance for us independent of the way they 'happen' to think, nor do their thoughts exist for us independently of the way they 'happen' to be put in whatever they say and do on the stage. On the contrary, their human reality, their status as characters, lies precisely in what they *acknowledge* this or that situation, person, relationship, object, question, or whatever, to be: in what they take their world to be, that is, as they give it substance in the words and deeds by which they confront and act upon it. Lear, for instance, is not a pre-existing person for us (as he is for Kent, say) to whom Shakespeare has given insights to see (and for us to see with him), as if Lear existed apart from what he acknowledges, or as if we already knew these to be valid insights before the play leads us to acknowledge them as such. Nor in the case of Shakespeare himself does the meaning of his play consist in a number of pre-existing insights or truths, which we already know to be truths and could see for ourselves if we looked hard enough, which Shakespeare is drawing to our attention, and which he personally endorses by making his hero eventually come to see them. The tissue of words and actions of which the various characters are created, and the total dramatic action comprising them all, are not a contingent, dispensable device by which Shakespeare tries to tell us his thoughts about life. There is no such device whose artistic 'success' we could somehow measure, any more than we could somehow measure the 'profundity' or 'truth' of Shakespeare's thoughts by reference to philosophers and theologians. His insights do not exist for us independently of the way he 'happened' to put them (and it is unlikely, to say the least, that they existed in any such way for him either). They exist *as* insights only as what he 'sees', or more strictly, in what he causes us to 'see', or more strictly still, in what his art makes us acknowledge the reality to be. They are only truths or insights in so far as their dramatic medium as a whole realizes them as such. No single character, however noble, however much he is wronged by others, however much he suffers, however close to death, can be treated as a privileged device to 'see' what Shakespeare meant to say in the play; nor can the meaning of the play lie in the meaning any single character comes to 'see' in his own experience. That meaning is to be found in no less than everything in the dramatic world we have to acknowledge as both real and true to our sense of common life, and it consists in whatever we have to acknowledge its full substance and shape to be. And one basic reality, which we never lose touch with, is that of the characters – what they say, and what they do, and what *they* mean by their words and deeds. But of course their reality to us is not their reality to themselves. To us, it lies in what they acknowledge at every point and in the visible facts of their doing so – in the content of what they 'see', in the manner in which they 'see' it, the reasons impelling them to 'see' it that way, and what they do in response to what they 'see' – all of which in turn are to be found only in the specific words and deeds that embody their particular forms and pressures *as* characters even while also evoking the forms and pressures of the world they inhabit and act upon.

II

None of this is particularly new, of course; it is only to recall what has been either said or implied by others, and especially by three Shakespeare critics to whom I (for one) am conscious of more debts than I could hope to acknowledge in detail, even though disagreeing with their particular views of *King Lear* as a whole: Arthur Sewell, L. C. Knights, and G. Wilson Knight. Each of these has moved beyond 'Bradleyism' towards a more adequate conception of 'character' and of its inseparable connection with the poetry; each, moreover, sees the necessity of viewing each play as an organic whole, a whole in which no part or aspect is supposed to dominate the rest. Yet strangely enough, when we examine their views of *King Lear* in particular, they all seem in dealing with it to have unwittingly accepted another of Bradley's assumptions – this time about the relationship between 'character' and the dramatic 'action' – without scrutinizing it as critically as their own arguments might and should have led them to do. And the paradoxical result is that even here other doors are opened to confusions about 'seeing'.

In the first chapter of his book, *Character and Society in Shakespeare*, for example, Arthur Sewell sees that the relevant conception of character in Shakespearean tragedy is 'by no means the self as the psychologists understand it; it is the moral self, which expresses itself in volition and is not to be usefully interpreted in terms of motivation'[1] – though, in justice to the rest of Sewell's argument, he probably does not mean 'motivation' here (since we clearly often must and do interpret characters' motives) so much as 'psychological laws' or 'causation'. More specifically, he continues, character consists in a particular vision of, or 'address' to, the world, a particular way of seeing and experiencing it, which also involves 'the way in which we apprehend [the character] in relation to the world, and, perhaps, the kind of world in which he is so apprehended'. It is discovered to us in incident and situation, for example, which are ideally 'catalysts by means of which, in character, vision

[1] Sewell, *Character and Society in Shakespeare*, p. 3.

is released, embodied, and enriched'.[1] But it is chiefly discovered

> in the mode in which the person of the play embodies in prose or poetry a distinctive address to the world . . . [Imagining] such an address involves also the imagining of a world – not a world specified by matters of fact, but a world of quality in which each matter of fact is something more than accidental . . .
>
> Character is individualized in imagery, because imagery creates the world as the character apprehends it and appropriates it – or rather, as the author imagines, in one activity, the character and the world as that character perceives it. Indeed, the matter is less straightforward even than this. For the language the character speaks is very often the poetic equivalent of his 'nature'; and his 'nature' is his characteristic address to the world, and this is nothing but the manner in which he discovers and engages his world in speech. But the poetic equivalent is generated by the dramatist within the situation. In all this, what we are really affirming is that there is no prose rendering for the poetically-conceived character, just as the paraphrase is never the poetry.[2]

This, with its reference to *the* 'nature' of the character, implies a conception of character that seems curiously (and, I think, significantly) fixed and static, but it does state one crucial point very succinctly. And Sewell does observe that the action of the play has at least to bring into 'more poignant relationship the character's way of meeting his world and the comprehensive vision of the play': only so can that vision be 'released and enriched, so that the particular case is apprehended in terms of the general case of Man'.[3]

Clearly, Sewell is trying to get beyond a wholly 'Bradleyan' conception of character and of its function in Shakespearean tragedy. It is, as he sees, a necessary but special kind of artistic convention, an imaginative *means*. Moreover, he sees that the total vision of the play requires a number of characters:

[1] *Ibid.*, pp. 21, 23.   [2] *Ibid.*, pp. 26–7, 29–30.   [3] *Ibid.*, p. 36.

the essential process of character-creation is a prismatic breaking-up of the comprehensive vision of the play; and each element of vision, so separated out, is in itself a unique illumination, finding its individual fulfilment in character.[1]

This makes an important point – or rather, it suggests it, for Sewell's terms are suspiciously scientific. What with 'prisms' and 'elements', the 'comprehensive vision of the play' also comes to seem a rather fixed and static thing, as though it somehow existed prior to, or in some way above, its realization in and by the play – just as a character's 'nature' seemed a rather fixed and static thing, as though it were merely one, definably 'individualized' element in the author's 'vision'. Sewell is right to insist on the sense in which character is an artistic means; in doing so, however, he does seem to forget the sense in which it is not – the sense, that is, in which the characters in a Shakespearean tragedy, however sketchily drawn, must seem to us autonomous beings whose nature and fate are not predetermined by some idea in the author's mind. That, indeed, is the precondition of their dramatic force and relevance, and actually to treat them as mere 'facets' or 'elements of vision' would be to dehumanize the drama, if not to denature it completely. This may be why, having seen that a range of characters is necessary to the dramatic action even if the action does not require they be all equally fully drawn, Sewell tends in practice to concentrate on the one figure whose character and fate cannot possibly be treated as predetermined in this way: the hero. Only by assuming that the hero is a special case can he put drama back into the 'comprehensive vision', as it were; yet in doing so he evades his own point, that the experience or 'vision' of *any* character in the drama, including the hero, is a vital part, but only a

[1] *Ibid.*, pp. 19–20.

46

part, of the whole. That remains valid even in Sewell's terms; and as it stands, his argument surely offers grounds enough to be wary of the basic Bradleyan assumption, that a Shakespearean tragedy is always (as Bradley himself put it) 'pre-eminently the story of one person, the "hero"'. That was the point from which Bradley went on to claim that 'the centre of the tragedy, therefore, may be said with equal truth to lie in action issuing from character, or in character issuing in action', and so to assume that the essential course of the tragedy is a series of changes in the hero's character or soul.[1]

The question here is not whether the hero is the central character in the drama – he is, by definition – but whether the dramatic *action* consists of his story, or more specifically, given the importance of the characters' consciousness or 'vision', whether the action consists essentially of the changes effected in the hero's consciousness or of those effected in ours. Of course the two are not opposed nor even wholly separate; on the other hand, they are by no means identical nor even exactly parallel. Clearly, we neither wholly identify with any character's vision nor, in so far as we have to understand it, are we wholly detached from it. To suppose that our vision moves only parallel with Lear's, for example, would be to assume that the meaning of the play – what it brings *us* to acknowledge – is pretty much what we see it bring Lear to acknowledge: to locate the essential action, that is, in the hero's consciousness (as if it were an arena of vicarious experience, into which we are drawn, and remain, by a virtually passive sympathy), rather than in the development of our consciousness, which necessarily has to range over much more from start to finish, and which is therefore engaged in continuous activity.

[1] Bradley, *Shakespearean Tragedy*, pp. 7, 12.

The term 'action' is notoriously ambiguous. It can refer to such different aspects of a play as what its characters do, for example, or to its narrative or plot, or to the skeletal pattern of its events, and so on.[1] In the most comprehensive sense, however, while it includes all of these, it must finally refer to the way the comprehensive vision of the play, of which all these are the medium, comes to be acknowledged by us *as* its comprehensive vision. That vision is not there for us merely to 'see', as if it existed apart from our progressively coming to accept it as real and valid or true, any more than 'insights' are merely given to the characters to 'see' in that way. The assumption that it is – in other words, a too fixed and static notion of it – leaves us with either a mere sequence of events that simply 'reveal' it, or the development of the hero's (or some other character's) insight, as the only truly *developing* aspect the play offers us. A more adequate conception of 'character' than Bradley's

[1] I trust that the general argument of this chapter, and particularly the sense in which I think we have to understand 'dramatic action', will sufficiently explain why I disagree with Robert Langbaum's argument in chapter 5 ('Character versus Action in Shakespeare') of his book, *The Poetry of Experience*, London, 1957. While thoroughly endorsing his general point – that a Shakespearean tragedy cannot be interpreted as the 'vision' of its dominant character – I cannot accept his claim that *either* we understand characters 'sympathetically', from within, and therefore (according to Langbaum) dissolve the drama into a merely relativistic or a merely psychological exhibition, *or* we understand the characters as being no more or less than the agents required by the plot, and the plot itself as the objective expression of an objective moral order. This seems to me a totally false dilemma. (Nor am I persuaded that it is only a 'modern' habit to understand Shakespeare's characters 'sympathetically'.) Langbaum's argument surely confuses 'plot' with the *action* of which it is an element, and the objectivity of a moral meaning *created* by, and in, an imaginative work, with the objectivity of a moral code that any writer may restate or re-affirm. I can see nothing peculiar to the *plot* of any Shakespearean tragedy that makes either the plot or the play a mere restatement of some pre-existing moral order – an order that we can suppose (whatever we think of it ourselves) Shakespeare accepted and then set about translating into theatrical terms.

requires a correspondingly more adequate conception of 'dramatic action'.

Thus for all that Sewell recognizes that we view the hero's nature and address to the world objectively, that all the other characters are dramatically important as well, that situation and incident and (above all) the poetic medium itself, constitute the meaningful substance of the play for us, his limiting conceptions both of character and of the play's 'comprehensive vision' lead him eventually to suggest that our awareness moves *only* in parallel with the hero's:

character is moral vision getting to know itself . . . the process by which vision discovers itself in character is a process of catharsis, and the purification that leaves the hero serene for death is at one with the purification which we ourselves must know . . . the hero undergoes an experience which puts all our previous attitude into question and which extracts from us, as from him, a transformation of vision which can accommodate and appropriate the new and un-covenanted experience.[1]

Consequently, for Sewell the essential movement of our vision in *King Lear* is towards 'seeing' what the main characters come to 'see': 'from conduct (and character) in which reason is governed by self-regard, to conduct (and character) in which reason is transformed by compassion'.[2] This suggests that anybody already capable of compassion will find it rather a dull play, just as those who see it as the process of Lear's redemption or salvation will find it a rather comforting one; but more importantly, it leaves us still with the prime difficulty of this play in particular, which is simply that the final catastrophe does not fulfil any visible logic in the movement of the hero's awareness

---

[1] Sewell, *Character and Society in Shakespeare*, pp. 60, 73, 75.
[2] *Ibid.*, p. 116.

at all. It does not extract from him any 'transformation' of vision or consciousness. On the other hand, this does not mean it does not fulfil some logic in the movement of ours. The two do not necessarily move in unison. Indeed, *King Lear* is an especially significant case precisely because any account of what is 'revealed' will always have to dispose of its ending in a more or less arbitrary way so long as it is assumed that the movement of our awareness has been virtually that of Lear's.

III

Interestingly enough, another form of the same sub-Bradleyan assumption haunts L. C. Knights's account of *King Lear* too. Like Sewell, though much more firmly and usefully, Knights has propounded a view of Shakespearean 'character' that is a decided advance on Bradley's. 'Character', he has insisted, is essentially the embodiment of a 'spiritual and psychological state with which the given experience is confronted', or more accurately, the embodiment of a 'possibility of living', a way of encountering the universe; and it is at once expressed and criticized both in the poetry given to the character to speak and in the dramatic interplay of such 'possibilities' with each other. To have seen this and stated it so clearly is itself a notable contribution to our understanding of Shakespeare; and as Knights has argued, it means that we must treat the tragedies as 'imaginative wholes rather than as dramatic constructions designed to exhibit "character", however fascinating', and not allow 'conventional "sympathy for the hero" . . . to distort the pattern of the whole'.[1]

[1] L. C. Knights, *An Approach to 'Hamlet'* (London, 1960), p. 34, cf. p. 14; 'The Question of Character in Shakespeare', in *Further Explorations* (London, 1965), p. 200; and 'How Many Children Had Lady Macbeth?' in *Explorations* (London, 1958 [1946]), p. 36.

Many of Knights's observations in *Some Shakespearean Themes* about the relationship between Lear's 'vision' and his particular substance as a character are consequently very much to the point:

Now if there is one truth that [*King Lear*] brings home with superb force it is that neither man's reason nor his powers of perception function in isolation from the rest of his personality: *quantum sumus, scimus. How* Lear feels, in short, is as important as *what* he feels, for the final 'seeing' is inseparable from what he has come to be.[1]

Or, in a more general but even more suggestive passage:

Shakespeare, then, does not say that 'nature, however inscrutable, is basically beneficent'; he does not say that there is 'in nature a core of tenderness which lies even deeper than pride or cruelty'. He says – though it takes the whole of *King Lear* to say it adequately – that nature *per se* is something quite other than human nature, and that it cannot properly be conceived in human terms; that its humanly relevant quality only exists in relation to a particular human outlook and standpoint; and what that quality is depends on the standpoint from which the relation is established. 'Nature-as-beneficent' is a concept that only has meaning for the good man – or at all events for the man who admits the imperatives of his own humanity. Perhaps it is easier to grasp this in relation to the world – the given 'nature' – of inner experience. The mind ('that ocean, where each kind Does straight its own resemblance find') contains within itself elements corresponding to non-human life – Blake's tiger and lamb. So long as these natural forces are not integrated by the specifically human principle they are, or are likely to become, chaotic and destructive. Given that principle, they may be sublimated and transformed, but they are not disowned: they are freely accepted as the natural sources of life and power.[2]

These are insights of considerable importance, I believe, both for Shakespeare and for other writers, though perhaps more in their implications than exactly as formulated here.

---

[1] Knights, *Some Shakespearean Themes*, p. 100.
[2] *Ibid.*, p. 132.

The first passage, reiterating and applying a point Sewell had touched on, puts in a nutshell why the metaphor of 'sight' should be so frequent in *Lear*. For if the relevant identity of a character, his 'self' as far as the play is concerned with it, exists for him in his conscious awareness of himself, it exists for us even more significantly in his awareness of everything *other* than himself – that is, in whatever he supposes (supposes even un-selfconsciously) himself merely to see. 'As a man is, so he sees', as Blake put it. And this principle, *King Lear* suggests again and again, applies to us (and to Shakespeare) as well as to the characters. The metaphor of 'sight' directs us not only to what the characters see (as Robert Heilman assumes in his book, *This Great Stage*), but to the fact and the manner of their 'seeing' – to what they are as human beings, and beyond that to the whole dramatic world the characters compose, to everything *we* are given to see but whose reality and meaning are only what we can and must acknowledge them to be. In the second passage Knights applies this same point to one dramatically crucial 'reality' – the various characters' conceptions of Nature and, beyond that again, to any conception we ourselves seek as Shakespeare's own. As Knights suggests, these are important precisely, but only, because they extend the same principle to whatever is acknowledged as the most basic, most comprehensive, and least contingent 'reality'.

Before turning to an especially relevant consequence of this second point, however, it may be worth noting one possible source of confusion. In developing his argument, Knights draws specifically on ideas which either derive directly from Coleridge or which (in part at least) entered English criticism mainly through him. At first glance, therefore, it may look merely anachronistic to approach Shakespeare through such Romantic (or Idealist) insights. Even if it were, of course, that would not make it absurd to apply those insights heuristically; nevertheless, as Knights's quotation from Marvell may remind us, not to mention Coleridge's own interest in seventeenth-century neo-platonism, similar insights were hardly unfamiliar to Shakespeare's age, even though it thought about them in a different metaphysical language. Indeed, formal ideas aside, it hardly takes much mother-wit to notice some relevant facts about human beings: that those with jaundiced eyes tend to see a jaundiced world, for instance, or that one needs good humour to see the comic side of things, or that a tyrant who looks for enemies all round him generally finds them all right. The point is one that a dramatist interested in men and women, and the words and images of the world by which they live in it, might even find himself pondering about his own tendencies too. But at a rather more abstract level, it is surely the same point that underlies some of the common beliefs of the time, especially those that ultimately derive from neo-platonic thought: the correspondence of inner microcosm and outer macrocosm, for example, or the notion that the cosmic harmony can only be heard by a man who is himself 'harmonically composed', or the rather more learned, but readily accessible, belief in the creative power of the soul to constitute its world anew and to make nature over as 'golden'. Such notions only become beliefs when they seem convincing answers to real questions; and for the Elizabethans they were clearly more than odd fancies washed up out of the past, which they could use to point a moral or adorn a tale. That literary historians often treat them as if they were only that, despite giving them the name of beliefs, only means that the thoughts of any age are bound to seem dead curiosities unless we realize the thinking embodied in them; and thinking is performed, more or less effectively, by individual minds. (Thus it is hard to believe that Shakespeare was so much more intellectually lazy and inept than those modern scholars, who, though they might treat Plato or Aquinas, say, with respectful caution, find no difficulty in locating *his* stock of 'ideas' or 'beliefs'. Nor is it likely that any common ideas or beliefs of the time were, for all literary-critical purposes, pretty much the same in Shakespeare's mind as in that of his local butcher.)

In any case, one obvious consequence of Knights's argument and (less obviously) of Sewell's too, is that we have to treat the various conceptions of 'Nature' and of 'the gods' expressed by the various characters in *King Lear* as essential components of the drama. Of course, as other critics have observed, each such conception reflects the character himself,[1] but Knights and Sewell suggest why and how this is so, and why therefore we have to take those conceptions seriously: for their import, that is, *within* the action. It is the action that both specifies and controls their significance. In other words, they are not given to us as beliefs to be detached from their specific dramatic contexts, philosophically considered, traced to parallel beliefs in other works of the time which settle their validity or invalidity, and then treated as signals of Shakespeare's own outlook, as if he must be simply endorsing the views he gives to his 'good' characters and rejecting those he gives to the 'bad' ones. Nor are the characters in *Lear* themselves philosophers, even of merely amateur status. Their conceptions of Nature or the gods do not define consciously formulated abstract posi-

---

[1] E.g. J. C. Maxwell, 'The Technique of Invocation in *King Lear*', *Modern Language Review*, XLV (1950), 142. William R. Elton's book, *King Lear and the Gods* (San Marino, 1968), also bears on the same point, though with awesome scholarly weight and a persistent tendency to treat the characters as if they were mouthpieces of philosophical commonplaces.

tions, but rather express and manifest their human selves – and do so just as much as, but not more than, other things they say and do. For in such conceptions they are acknowledging the things and forces, among everything they acknowledge as objectively real, that seem to them most basic, most important, and (especially with 'the gods') most powerful and purposive. To select the salient contours of reality, the basic pattern or meaning or purpose manifest in it, is to evaluate; the order that is found (as 'Nature' or 'the gods') answers to the experience and the mind given to the search. 'Nature' is not like an object seen and then named, but like a truth, acknowledged in being named as such.

Needless to say, the selecting and evaluating implicit in the characters' conceptions of 'Nature' and 'the gods' are far more sharply visible to us, standing outside them as we do, than they could be to the characters themselves. We can notice how each conception relates and contrasts not only with others (within the play or outside it), but more importantly how it relates and contrasts with the individual character's other acts. There is much else in anybody's sense of reality than those things he can acknowledge as *most* real, as it were. His unconsidered turns of phrase, the unwitting drift of his actions, the impulsive movements of his tongue or his hand or his heart, betray an awareness of reality, to which each act itself is answering, but an awareness he is not reflexively conscious of. Just as his self differs from his consciousness of self, so those aspects of the world that are actually most basic and important to him differ from his present conception of them. Such conceptions are therefore an essential part of the drama in *King Lear* just because each of them, uttered at a particular time and place, expresses something of what the character makes of the reality he has been confronting in his experience; yet since the drama also includes the reality of the characters them-selves for us to experience, those conceptions cannot – any more than other truths the characters 'see' – be taken as the subject of the play. *King Lear* is not, in however subtle a way, essentially *about* competing philosophies of Nature expressed by or embodied in the characters, not is its essen-tial action merely an attempt to adjudicate between such philosophies.

And yet it is not easy to resist the temptation to seek the meaning of this play particularly, and hence to establish its value, in some rock-bottom, final truth -- some insight which is supposed to be already certified as 'true' and which is taken as 'final' because it is what the hero eventually comes to see. As in Sewell, this assumption lurks about the passages from Knights quoted above (and indeed about his account of *King Lear* as a whole). It is there in the special importance attached to Lear's 'final "seeing"' in the first passage for example, or in the phrase, '*the* specifically human principle', in the second (a principle that is surely less self-evident a datum than this implies). But it appears most clearly in the view that:

in the successive stripping away of the layers of experience, what remains to discover is the most fundamental reality of all. In the play it takes the form of the love and forgiveness of Cordelia . . .[1]

What I find difficult to accept here are not just the assump-tions implicit in '*the* most fundamental reality' and '*it* takes the form of . . .' but also those implicit in 'successive stripping away' and 'what remains to discover' – assump-tions that seem to me to produce or support a tacit, but quite drastic, oversimplification of the dramatic action and therefore an equally drastic understatement of other things,

[1] *Some Shakespearean Themes*, pp. 99–100.

very different from love and forgiveness, which the play makes us experience as equally 'fundamental' realities.

It is surprising that Knights should interpret *King Lear* in this way, since he places so much emphasis on Shakespeare's irony with other tragic heroes;[1] but his account of *Lear* seems to me weakened by its relative neglect of the process in which we acknowledge whatever moral order we find in the drama as an intelligible meaning, as truly moral, and as really and pervasively there. Knights does recognize (as many Shakespeare critics do not) that our judgment of character is

not a matter of formal approval or condemnation of a dramatic figure conceived as a real person . . . [but] essentially . . . part of an imaginative apprehension of life in which, with the whole force of our personality . . . we try to see fundamental aspects of human life in their true status and relationships. And what we judge, in this sense, is not someone 'out there', but potentialities of our own being.[2]

Moreover, he is fully aware that the action of *King Lear* consists of a 'complex interplay' of 'probings, questionings, rejections, recognitions'; that 'our capacity to see is dependent upon our capacity to feel'; and that the drama continuously 'enlivens and controls our sympathies and perceptions'.

King Lear is indeed, for most of the play, 'the centre of consciousness': what he sees we are forced to see. But the question, ultimately, is not what Lear sees but what Shakespeare sees, and what we, as audience, are prompted to see with him. At the end, however poignantly we may feel . . . we are still concerned with nothing less than the inclusive vision of the whole . . .[3]

[1] Cf. *An Approach to 'Hamlet'*, pp. 86, 89; and *Explorations*, p. 20, on the dramatic relevance of things not 'immediately relevant to the fortunes of the protagonist'.

[2] *An Approach to 'Hamlet'*, p. 50.

[3] *Some Shakespearean Themes*, pp. 113-14, 117-19.

As general statements, these seem both true and relevant; indeed, they put very concisely much of what I am trying to argue here. In practice, however, Knights's emphases seem to fall rather differently: on the 'true status and relationships' that are 'revealed' to us, rather than on the difficulties of 'trying' to locate them; on what we are forced to 'see' with Lear himself, rather than on what we are forced to see with Shakespeare, and not just 'ultimately', but right from the very beginning; on the 'positive values' we acknowledge rather than the divisions, doubts, and uncertainties with which we have to acknowledge them. The result is to make it seem once again, for all Knights's disclaimers, as if we go to the play more for the thoughts embodied in it than for the thinking – the highly complex experience in which (and only in which) the substance of the thought exists for us. In concentrating on the play as a 'pattern of moral evaluations',[1] Knights allows the evaluations to seem much easier, clearer and simpler than they are:

The imaginative discovery that is the play's essence has thus involved the sharpest possible juxtaposition of rival conceptions of 'Nature'. In the Edmund–Goneril–Regan group the philosophy of natural impulse and egotism has been revealed as self-consuming, its claim to represent strength as a self-bred delusion. What Lear touches in Cordelia, on the other hand, is, we are made to feel, the reality, and the values revealed so surely there are established in the face of the worst that can be known of man or Nature. To keep nothing in reserve, to slur over no possible cruelty or misfortune, was the only way of ensuring that the positive values discovered and established in the play should keep their triumphant hold on our imagination, should assert that unconditional rightness which, in any full and responsive reading of *King Lear*, we are bound to attribute to them.[2]

[1] *Further Explorations,* p. 201.
[2] *Some Shakespearean Themes,* pp. 117–18.

'Rival' conceptions of Nature; 'revealed' quickly becoming 'established'; 'delusion' set against 'the reality'; 'unconditional' rightness: terms like these surely make *King Lear* look simpler than it is. For even Edmund, Goneril and Regan embody 'potentialities of our own being'. Values are hardly 'established' merely by our having to 'feel' them as true or positive, while rival values are 'revealed' as 'delusions' because their proponents fail in their schemes. Nor do positive values stand in mere opposition to 'cruelty or misfortune'; surely they only become values in so far as they give moral significance to cruelty and suffering from as it were *within*? Unless we found it hard to dismiss the values of a Goneril or an Edmund as a mere delusion external to ourselves, and hard to trust to our inner, individual feelings about any kind of values, there would be little point in talking about values becoming 'established'. On the other hand, just because we do find it so hard, it is impossible to talk as if any values are 'established' conclusively.

To speak (as Knights does) of *King Lear* being directed towards 'affirmation *in spite of everything*'[1] therefore requires a full recognition not only of what is 'affirmed', but of what 'in spite of' means all the way through. Again, to speak of 'the imaginative discovery that is the play's essence' can all too easily suggest that the 'discovery', the moral pattern of the whole, is more important and more real than the human experience in which (and only in which) it exists at all – exists, that is, as more than a merely imagined artistic pattern, or an abstract and therefore arbitrary moral pattern. In *King Lear*, the process of discovering matters more, I think, than Knights's account seems to allow; and it matters just because it is always open,

[1] *Ibid.*, p. 119.

problematic, and therefore profoundly disturbing. More-over, it goes on throughout the play, from the beginning to the very end.

Of course, I do not suppose Knights would deny much of this; in fact, in his general remarks he points in the same direction himself. But his phraseology does at times seem to pull in another direction. In his essay on 'The Question of Character in Shakespeare', for example (where he argues explicitly against Bradley's view of tragedy as the story of the hero, and explicitly considers Sewell's views as well), he remarks that of the greater Shakespearean plays:

it is true to say that *all* the characters are necessary to express the vision – the emergent 'idea' or controlling preoccupation – and they are necessary only in so far as they do express it.[1]

But is the essential fixity of a word like 'idea' (or of the other word he uses, 'theme') qualified sufficiently by the adjective 'controlling' or 'emergent'? No such 'idea' or 'preoccupation' becomes 'vision' merely by emerging to someone's sight, nor merely by being felt as a controlling presence. Its reality and truth depend on much more than the dramatically central position of the character who seems to 'express' it most clearly or to whom it does seem to 'emerge':

Gloucester's part in *King Lear* is not to give additional human in-terest, but to enact and express a further aspect of the Lear experi-ence; for with Gloucester, as with Lear, confident acceptance of an inadequate code gives place to humble acceptance of the human condition, and there are glimpses of a new wisdom . . .[2]

We may well ask if this is an accurate description either of Gloucester or of his experience, and if it is not equally

---

[1] *Further Explorations*, p. 200.   [2] *Ibid.*

true to say that, in helping to create our total vision, Lear likewise enacts and expresses a further aspect of the Gloucester experience? Or to put the question another way, is not the play so hard to confront precisely because we have to see in Goneril, say, or Kent, in whom there are no such glimpses of a new wisdom, just as basic and irreducible a reality as in Cordelia?

IV

Much the same kind of question is provoked by Wilson Knight's account of *King Lear* too, I think, and again provoked partly by some of his own best insights. His attack in the first chapter of *The Wheel of Fire* on character-study and the 'ethical' kind of criticism it encourages, and his seminal conception of Shakespeare's plays in 'spatial' and metaphorical terms, are still highly relevant and (up to a point) convincing, despite his occasional confusion about the term 'character' and his natural enough tendency to overstate his case. Again, his account of the 'comedy of the grotesque' in *King Lear* is a brilliantly original and stimulating insight. The trouble arises, as I suggested above, from his use of the word 'reality' (or 'knowledge') in remarks like the following:

Each incident, each turn of thought, each suggestive symbol throughout *Macbeth* or *King Lear* radiates inwards from the play's circumference to the burning central core without knowledge of which we shall miss their relevance and necessity: they relate primarily, not directly to each other, nor to the normal appearances of human life, but to this central reality alone.[1]

For Wilson Knight, this 'central reality' is not just the centre of the drama. He assumes, or asserts, it to be a metaphysical reality as well, a 'burning core' of life itself, of

[1] Wilson Knight, *The Wheel of Fire*, p. 11.

which the drama is the direct record or expression, and which a critic of the play can therefore enable us simply to 'know'. The consequences for *King Lear* emerge in the second of his chapters on it, 'The Lear Universe'. Arguing, for example, that the 'mental atmosphere' of the play is a 'philosophic vision', he confuses the two senses of 'vision' or 'reality' in assuming that this atmosphere is not merely the most important *dramatic* reality it presents to our sight, but a most important – that is, valid – vision of reality itself. Even though he admits that this philosophic vision is 'true only within the scope of its own horizon',[1] he proceeds from the premiss that this vision comprehends everything visible within the horizon of the play, to the assumption that there is nothing else in our minds while we experience the play except what we are given to 'see' or to 'know' within its horizon. In other words, from the perfectly justified belief that we need to seek the meaning of the play as a whole, and that every aspect and detail of the play, including its poetic substance, is symbolic or expressive of that meaning, he tends to slide into the more questionable belief that everything is equally symbolic of it and symbolic to the same degree. In the end, he treats Shakespeare's 'vision' as if it existed in some transcendental way *behind* the play as we experience it, in some transcendental realm behind the world we supposedly share with the characters; and he treats the play as if it communicated or revealed that realm to us directly (if symbolically) in its 'vision'. Hence, for much of the time, Wilson Knight discusses the play as though any image, speech, or deed, by any character on any occasion, placed as well as any other that 'vision' directly in our sight. It is hard to discover by what means (if any) he supposes the truth of that vision is established

[1] *Ibid.*, p. 179.

to us, in what (if any) adjustments with what opposing possibilities it is validated *as* vision (and not fantasy or nightmare), or by what principles (if any) it is controlled.

Thus the human reality of the characters – the immediate, visible actuality of what they say and do in front of us – is virtually dissolved for Wilson Knight in the vision of 'nature' of which they, and everything else, are merely parts or aspects. He notices, for instance, that the references to 'the gods' in the play do not imply any belief in 'the gods' on Shakespeare's part: they are 'figments of the human mind'.[1]

The poet sees them as images in the minds of the dramatic persons, never as direct realities . . . The explicit religion blends therefore with the naturalistic outlook of the whole: gods and fiends are part of man and all are part of nature, merging with animals, elements, earth and its flowers.[2]

The first part of this is true; but instead of asking what would seem the obvious next questions – which gods and fiends are part of which man? and why? – Wilson Knight assimilates the kind of reality the characters have for us to the kind of reality animals and flowers and so on have for the characters. Whatever the eye of the poet sees is equally real or unreal in his comprehensive and transcendental 'vision'.

But what values are thus revealed to our sight, since what the poet sees for us must be more than a 'vision' of nature in the literal sense of the word? Wilson Knight's answer to this question is, as we might now expect, the least convincing part of his account. He talks of Edgar as 'so often the voice of the *Lear* philosophy', for example, or the way each character 'by suffering finds himself more truly, more surely knows the centre on which human fate revolves, more clearly sees the gods' mysterious

---

[1] *Ibid.*, p. 187.   [2] *Ibid.*, p. 189.

beneficence',[1] and so forth. Since meaning (a 'centre') has to be found in the play, and meaning can only be meaning to someone's consciousness, but since this 'vision' is also supposedly expressed *equally* in every aspect or detail, character or image, Knight is now free to locate the play's meaning in whatever consciousness on whatever occasion he pleases.

The way he discusses the ending of the play probably reveals this most clearly, just because, as he sees, the meaning of that cannot really be located in any character's consciousness of it. Lear, he has claimed, comes to see 'only with the eyes of love'; yet love is only 'the last reality but one in Lear's story: love and God. Not the last . . . There remains death . . . '[2] Having therefore to consider what the ending prompts in *our* consciousness, Wilson Knight finds himself in a familiar dilemma: 'Wherein shall we seek our revelation – in that deathless dream of love, or in this death?'[3] The choice of many critics goes to the latter, of course; Wilson Knight's goes to the former; though the dilemma only arises from the assumptions both sides share. Wilson Knight's basic argument for his choice is the assertion that 'on the wide canvas of this play three persons stand our with more vivid life than the rest: Edmund, Lear, Cordelia'.[4] The philosophical vision which the play is supposed to make us just see is tacitly identified with the dramatic reality it makes us just see; and the sheer arbitrariness of Wilson Knight's selection of characters that we supposedly 'see' most vividly betrays the assumptions behind it. For is Edmund's 'life' any more vivid to us than Goneril's or Albany's or Kent's? The universe does not 'travail and bring forth its miracle of love in them', but why are they therefore any the less real to us? That does not make them

[1] *Ibid.*, p. 197.   [2] *Ibid.*, p. 199.   [3] *Ibid.*, pp. 203–4.   [4] *Ibid.*, p. 200.

any the *more* real, of course; but whether we like it or not, we have to acknowledge the reality of other aspects than this not just of Edmund, but of Cordelia and of Lear too. ·

V

The objection here is not that to which many Christian or quasi-Christian or traditionally metaphysical interpretations of the play are open, and which H. A. Mason puts very briskly in his book on *Shakespeare's Tragedies of Love*:

the play will appear a very different thing to the man who finds Shakespeare merely echoing the great commonplaces of Christianity and to the man who if he wants to use the term 'religious' defines it in terms of this play and refuses to identify the terms Shakespeare uses and the same words as used by orthodox Christians. And bound up with this reflection is another: that the man who automatically identifies the terms without examining the contexts is not exposing himself to Shakespeare but accommodating Shakespeare to a preconceived view.[1]

L. C. Knights's interpretation and much of Wilson Knight's too, for example, are not simply imposing a preconceived view on the text. As I take it, the problem arises rather from expecting the play to disclose a basic 'truth' or 'insight' or 'fundamental reality' or 'value' for us merely to *see*, whether we supposedly see it in the texture of words and images, or reflected in the eyes of the hero. In fact, the same problem arises with Mason's own view of the play as well – a view that leads him to find a 'radical incoherence' in it.

The starting point of Mason's criticism seems to be the familiar belief that the action of the play is the spiritual development of Lear, and its meaning ought to lie in what he comes to see. Mason is quite right, I think, in his claim

[1] H. A. Mason, *Shakespeare's Tragedies of Love* (London, 1970), p. 166, n. 2.

that it does not really work like this; and having to discover someone who does develop spiritually from Act III
onwards, he turns instead to Gloucester. But he is left
troubled that Shakespeare seems to have 'no settled systems
of morality and religion to draw on'.

> The imagination is not satisfied whenever a deep draught is needed,
> as it is whenever we want to be sure that some ultimate value is
> being posited . . . What I am hankering for would be a few
> dramatic ultimates, things which cannot in the context of the fiction
> be questioned or made to look subordinate to anything else.[1]

This is an instructive case, for clearly Mason is not the
only one to hanker for that in literature, and to object when
he does not find it; though, considering that life itself does
not offer most of us 'ultimates . . . which cannot be questioned or made to look subordinate to anything else', we
may well wonder what conception of great tragic art would
lead one to require that *it* should. But Mason's criticism
here (not unlike Johnson's, or in another way the familiar
Bradleyan objection to the 'superfluous' characters and sub-
plot, to mention no others) seems to arise once again from
expecting Shakespeare to declare his ultimate meaning to
us, quite unequivocally, in some insight or state given the
hero to realize in his consciousness – whether or not it is
exactly specifiable as love and forgiveness, or wisdom, or
renunciation, or patience, or endurance, or redemption, or
compassion, or Truth, or something else – rather than expecting the play to declare its meaning as whatever its total
world gives *us* to realize. Shakespeare does satisfy our imagination, I believe, but not by trying to hand us his personal
values in that way, nor would it satisfy the imagination
even if he succeeded in doing so.

[1] *Ibid.*, p. 210.

What satisfies it is surely the dramatic reality he unfolds to our experience, and the meaning we have to *win* in it; and it satisfies, I would suggest, precisely in being so compelling that in order to hold the consciousness of it at all, we have to *search* for whatever we can and need to acknowledge as values. In other words, if we consider everything we are given merely to see, then probably the sole ultimate this exhibits is the continuous, pervasive, and eventually devastating condition of human experience itself, within which ultimate values (just like 'Nature', or 'the gods', or 'justice') are the answers *we* each have to give to questions we each *have* to ask – the very asking as well as the answering being the form in which we choose (as best we can) to take conscious possession of our experience.

3

The minor characters

—————

I

If the action of *King Lear* does not essentially consist in Lear's story that does not mean he is any the less the hero. It only means that, although he is at the centre of the play, neither his consciousness nor his experience comprehends all of its meaning; and further, that we cannot identify with him, or see him in a special, privileged way, or respond to him or his speeches with a different kind of sympathetic understanding and critical detachment from that with which we respond to anyone else. In fact, he is the hero for the same reasons as require us to acknowledge the reality, force, and limitations of the other characters in so far as they exist for us (in their varying degrees of density) as characters at all. His 'heroism' requires their specific selves as its very condition. The terms on which they enter into the action *as* characters are those examined most profoundly and thoroughly in Lear – in what is at issue in his self and his experience, in his particular 'address' or 'stance' towards his world, and what his transactions with it reveal about the world that he, and his world, and the other characters' transactions, constitute for us. Each of the other characters, being composed by the same creative activity out of the same material as he, though in a way that testifies to his larger stature and vitality, unfolds a kind of commentary on him – as he on them. What makes them essential elements in the action is that each embodies, however sketchily, a possible form of life within the same world they share with Lear – a possibility *we* have to understand and come to terms with. But we can do this only by grasping each possibility in its mutual bearings with the others, and beyond that, its mutual bearings with those embodied in Lear himself.

Kent offers probably the simplest example: a figure unlike Lear in his simple, direct, unquestioningly loyal attachments to others and his equally simple, direct, unquestioningly loyal attachment to a firmly held sense of himself; like Lear, however, in his need to sustain a sense of himself, and a sense of reality or 'Nature', whose strength depends on its defensive limits; and yet unlike him again in that the limits are so narrow and rigid that he cannot imagine, much less assimilate, any experience that breaches them. The condition of Kent's virtue is one (pretty limited) kind of self-abnegation – an abnegation of the merely selfish or self-seeking – and its product one (pretty limited) kind of patience. But while these qualities form an obvious comment on Lear's case, as of course on others in the play, they are in turn commented upon, and most notably by Lear's. Regarded in isolation, as a figure of Shakespeare's imagination, Kent is only a relatively simple 'character'; regarded as part of the total action, however, that is as part of the dramatic reality of which he is a fully created element, his character is that of a relatively simple man. He is one who positively needs to give his loyalty in order to be the person he is, to attach himself to a straightforward, clear-cut, more powerful good outside himself that can command his full allegiance.

LEAR . . . What would'st thou?
KENT Service . . .
LEAR Dost thou know me, fellow?

KENT No, Sir; but you have that in your countenance
     which I would fain call master.
LEAR What's that?
KENT Authority.   (I, iv, 24–32)

The turn of that is characteristic of Kent throughout. He
is not the kind of man who could really 'know' Lear, of
course: how to feel, how to think, how to act, never become
problems for him. For him, Cordelia in the first scene 'justly
think'st and hast most rightly said', and therefore she
deserves only that 'the Gods to their dear shelter take thee'
(I, i, 182–3). At the same time Lear is still for him his master
whom he loves, the 'old kind King'. To Kent, Lear's sufferings are definable in quite straightforward terms: 'a
sovereign shame [that] elbows him', 'his own unkindness',
'a burning shame', and so on. The kind of conscious honesty
he lives by is the quality he most values in others: 'I know,
sir, I am no flatterer'. Truth is simply a coin of a certain
value and he simply a man who takes it and passes it on
without deceit.

And yet Cornwall does almost make a point, however
unwittingly, when he sneers that

> This is some fellow,
> Who, having been prais'd for bluntness, doth affect
> A saucy roughness, and constrains the garb
> Quite from his nature: he cannot flatter, he,
> An honest mind and plain, he must speak truth . . .
>   (II, ii, 96–100)

The real point is not that Kent is anything less than he
claims to be; he does serve the authority of goodness, and
that involves no constraint of his garb from his nature.
It is rather that he is not much more than he claims to be:
his nature – his very capacity to feel and to act – seems constrained by his very virtues, his ethical character. His

attack on Oswald in this scene is a telling comment in itself: he evidently feels free to let his aggression loose (admittedly on a figure who has invited something for his insolence to Lear) as if his moral responsibility for it were entirely subsumed by a larger authority outside himself – partly that of his master and partly that of his own virtuous principles.) (When this man, who has beaten Oswald with his sword, accompanied by the man who has actually killed him later on, kneels before the broken-hearted Lear at the end, Lear's distracted reply also unwittingly makes a point: 'A plague upon you, *murderers*, traitors all!')

The tone and accent of Kent's speech all through the play are obviously 'stoic' – plain, rather terse, unambiguous, without much metaphoric complexity. It is a language not much *open* to experience; indeed, it is usually tightened around its virtue like a fist in order to oppose the world. Latent in it is a kind of aggressive defensiveness. The way Kent experiences the storm in Act III, for instance, is revealing:

> . . . the wrathful skies
> Gallow the very wanderers of the dark,
> And make them keep their caves. Since I was a man
> Such sheets of fire, such bursts of horrid thunder,
> Such groans of roaring wind and rain, I never
> Remember to have heard; man's nature cannot carry
> Th'affliction nor the fear.   (III, ii, 43–9)

Human nature and the elements, like good and bad, or truth and falsity, or the party of right and the party of wrong, are essentially clear-cut opponents as Kent sees them, and the one has to batten itself down to survive the assaults of the other. In difficulties, his mind always turns to the idea of sheer endurance; as the rest of Act III underlines, however, endurance is a different way of coping with life from actually suffering it. The earlier interchange, in Act II scene iv, between Kent (enduring punishment in the stocks) and the Fool had already contrasted the unreflective, undivided, almost self-satisfied virtue of the one with the sardonic self-division of the other, who can sustain his loyalty to Lear only by insisting on the lack of commonsense wisdom in it.

> KENT Where learn'd you this, Fool?
> FOOL Not i' the stocks, Fool. (II, iv, 86–7)

Thus the kind of 'justice' Kent looks for is apparently quite simple and straightforward, corresponding to the apparently quite simple possibility of moral order he represents in the play. Needless to say, that it is simple and straightforward is no disadvantage in itself; on the contrary, it is precisely what makes both Kent and the kind of justice he wants seem so attractive to many readers – it is part of what we want too. The only trouble is that we can also recognize it as too simple – or rather, as simple in the wrong way. It is too external, too abstract, and yet too much directed to confirming the self-enclosed ego. What Kent looks for as he endures is the inevitable turn of Fortune's wheel that will 'give/Losses their remedies' (II, ii, 169ff). It is the stoic's trust, not in the individual's capacity so to experience the world that the experience re-shapes the very terms on which the world exists for him, but in an external cosmic justice that is rather like a mechanically self-adjusting balance – an objective, cosmic law corresponding to what Coleridge has called 'debtor and creditor principles of virtue' in the individual.[1] Beside the out-going pity and indignation with which Cordelia thinks of 'mine enemy's dog', for instance, Kent's is significantly different when a similar image comes to his mind:

[1] Cited by Knights, *Some Shakespearean Themes*, p. 94 n.

> Why, Madam, if I were your father's dog,
> You should not use me so.   (II, ii, 136-7)

After Gloucester has helped Lear to the hovel in the storm, it is Kent who remarks, 'The Gods reward your kindness!' (III, vi, 5). A man has a right to expect payment for what is due to him: an attitude that turns as readily to a self-protective indignation as to a certain kind of patience.

That losses are not given their remedies – that Kent is put in the stocks like a dog, that Gloucester is immediately 'rewarded' by having his eyes torn out, that Cordelia's return brings only defeat – is one obvious comment the play makes about such human wishes as Kent's. The relationship between his will, with its potential violence, and, that of Goneril, Regan and Cornwall is another. For Kent the sight of the dead Cordelia in Lear's arms causes the whole structure of his world to break apart: 'Is this the promis'd end?' Endurance now seems to him to have been pointless all along, since the only point it had lay in some expected future vindication, in a morally intelligible Final Judgment. If this is it, there is no reckoning, no promised justice, and the world's rack is too tough. All is too 'cheerless, dark, and deadly' for him to endure any longer. A follower to the last, he surrenders his fate to the authority of Lear's: 'My master calls me, I must not say no'. In short, rather like Dr Johnson confronting Shakespeare's play, it is not so much the vanity of human wishes he cannot endure, as being denied any justification for what had seemed to be given to humanity from outside in order to *be* endured. Nevertheless, if such ideas of 'justice' as Kent's seem unsophisticated, they are surely, as Johnson claimed, also natural. Justice is at bottom a kind of civilized revenge, and although an eye for an eye may strike us as too uncivilized a form of it (though clearly it doesn't strike everybody that way), the scales still have to be balanced by some given and recognizable system of measurement. In other words, Shakespeare does not encourage us to stand aloof from such 'debtor and creditor' principles as Kent's (or Johnson's), let alone dismiss them as impossibly crude. On the contrary. It is just because we do respond to them as natural that they become so much of a problem for us as we respond to other possibilities.

II

While Kent is thus something more than a case of Elizabethan stoicism, Edmund is something more than a case of Elizabethan naturalism. He is not given much density as a figure after his first major scene (I, ii), but since his particular way of trying to master life is by manipulating it, what he does – or rather, what he progressively wills himself to dare – is more revealing than anything he could say. For many readers, the most striking thing about him is his amoral, a-social conception of nature; in fact, he too thinks this the most striking thing about himself. For he is, we notice, the first to point out his own cleverness and boldness of thought. Even at first glance we surely recognize him as one of that familiar type, the consciously 'brilliant' young man on the make, and the cheap naturalistic commonplaces he flashes about are obviously self-fortifying rationalizations rather than a deeply pondered 'philosophy' that requires all the resources of scholarly criticism (aided, of course, by Shakespeare's dramatic skill) to expose. What is interesting about them is not their validity or invalidity as beliefs, but the kind of inner weakness that needs them. As a figure in the total design of the play, Edmund's cold, hypocritical unscrupulousness obviously relates him with Goneril and Regan, and helps to broaden our sense of a 'fateful malignant influence' abroad in the world of the play, as Bradley put it. In other ways, however, he is also related with Lear and Kent and Gloucester, and helps to broaden our sense of the subtle kinships of that world.

As the action unfolds, it becomes clear that, however much Edmund drives his will towards socially acknowledged position and power, it always drives him to self-concealment. He cannot say anything to another person that is not false; more to the point, he is driven to be just as false to himself. Even in his reply to Goneril's declaration of love – 'Yours in the ranks of death' (IV, ii, 25) – his tone seems to see-saw over some inner emptiness, an incapacity to know how much, if anything, he means. One of the sharpest ironies is the obvious truth of his reply, for there *is* almost nothing left alive in him (or in her, for that matter) except unenlightened self-interest and an energetic, machine-like will to serve it. The very qualities of his opening soliloquy in Act I, scene ii – so frankly 'honest', so 'lively', so engagingly 'clever' – positively invite us, in the context of the first scene between Lear and Cordelia, to notice how much they serve to conceal from himself. His first words, for instance, place nature outside him, as wholly external – a 'goddess' to whose law his services are 'bound' – and once again such assumptions are quickly revealed as part and parcel of a conception of the self at once defensive and mutilating. In one sense of the phrase, the 'composition and fierce quality' Edmund obviously wants are visible in his speech. It seems full of life; but the vitality is brittle, over-concentrated, over-conscious, as if wrought over by a will straining to make itself as pure and free as possible, uncontaminated by any spot of weakness. And of course his weakness is precisely that strain. For all his liveliness, he is wound up tight with social resentment, which admittedly he can acknowledge, but also with a consuming envy of Edgar which he cannot quite fully acknowledge. Far from being strong, in fact, he has to talk himself into a feeling of strength ('I grow, I prosper . . .') – or at least of such strength as protects him from the fear and insecurity we infer behind so much envy. Being driven by forces whose implications for his own moral being he cannot acknowledge and which therefore seem almost uncontrollable, inevitably he sees nature as a similar but amoral conflict of forces and, in the same process, sees himself as constrained to deny himself not only all morality but all the feelings from which morality grows. It is a familiar enough pattern.

Edmund is too sharp-witted, however, merely to suppose that nature *forces* him to be wicked or self-seeking. He despises his father – indeed, all men – for needing just such comforting delusions as that:

This is the excellent foppery of the world . . . as if we were villains on necessity, fools by heavenly compulsion . . . and all that we are evil in, by a divine thrusting on. An admirable evasion of whoremaster man, to lay his goatish disposition to the charge of a star! . . . Fut! I should have been that I am had the maidenliest star in the firmament twinkled on my bastardizing. (I, ii, 124ff)

The significant thing about Edmund's mockery is not his bright, 'tough-minded' wit, but the hard contempt for human weakness informing the wit – a contempt so determined not to yield weakness an inch (especially in his father) that it seems to be whipping down any suspicion of it in himself. He can see nothing in external reality to support men in their need to think well of themselves (even when they cannot act well) because he can feel nothing in himself to support it. And in filling that void with the more obvious reality of his own ego, he can feel that he *chooses* his 'realism' and that it is a mark of his superiority to do so.

What is more, though, he can also satisfy the same 'weakness', the same need, in himself without having to acknowledge it, by supposing the amorality of nature constrains him not to wickedness but to a detached, 'realistic' independence. What he takes as reality outside himself is the sanction as well as the counterpart of what he reduces himself to. The 'law' he sees as nature's, and so feels (morally, as it were) obliged to serve, is one that obliges him (of necessity, as it were) to crystallize every possibility of his own nature in ruthless will, to *be* nothing except what serves that will. In that way he can possess himself in a flawless, impregnable, objective integrity.

Edmund is one who conspicuously does receive 'justice' – a self-produced nemesis. It has an especially appropriate form, in fact, if there is to be glimpsed (as I think there is) behind his resentment and envy and will to power, the need (which he has to deny as a 'weakness') for a reassuring affection ('Our father's love is to the bastard Edmund / As to th'legitimate' (I, i, 17–18)), and with that need a fear, which again he cannot face or even name, that he might not be much of a man after all and specifically not as much of one as Edgar. At any rate Edgar comes to him both nameless and faceless, and defeats him in an open conflict of force – a conflict of just the kind to which Edmund has bound his will. There is at least a double irony in Goneril's exclamation as he falls:

> By th'law of war thou wast not bound to answer
> An unknown opposite; thou art not vanquish'd,
> But cozen'd and beguil'd.   (V, iii, 152–4)

In one sense Goneril is right; yet in another sense of the word, Edmund's will has always been bound to do it, since it has always been driven by the need to prove his identity.

And the moral point Goneril unconsciously makes in 'cozen'd and beguil'd' (for who did the cozening?) is not at all lessened by the fine irony of moral indignation in *her* mouth. Again, when he has to recognize his defeat, he resorts to exactly the same self-deluding 'weakness' he had derided in others. Where Edgar (characteristically) sees Edmund's fate in terms of a simple moral pattern – the gods making our vices instruments to plague us – Edmund turns to the equally simple but significantly more mechanical image: 'The wheel is come full circle; I am here' – as though *it* had brought him there and the fact of his defeat proved the existence and power of the wheel. We cannot put much weight on any of this in Act V, of course, or on his final repentance: it is only sketchily drawn, and heavily overshadowed by more important things. But if there is a touch of very revealing pathos in his 'Yet Edmund was belov'd . . .', there is an equally revealing note of simple self-respect in it that he has never used before. This next sentence, if it is motivated at all, seems to flow from that:

> I pant for life; some good I mean to do
> Despite of mine own nature.

The connection between life and self-respect – in the sense of being able to accept even one's own human weakness – seems to me at the centre of the figure of Edmund; in another sense of the phrase, he might be said to have always panted for them. As an element in the over-all design, he is as close to Lear and Cordelia as to Goneril and Regan.

III

Where father and daughter stand juxtaposed in the first scene, so father and son are in the second. This is not to say, however, that the so-called sub-plot merely duplicates the main one: it does not; and although it is often said or implied, I for one remain unconvinced that Shakespeare had to repeat the story of a credulous father and an unloving child in order to intensify and universalize a story he surely makes intense and universal enough in itself. The similarities between the two sets of figures ought not to distract attention from the differences between them, which are probably more important in the end – so much so, indeed, that unless we attend to them sufficiently the action seems to cut no wider or deeper than does the main plot, and Lear's experience appears not merely to dominate but in effect to circumscribe our interest and the meaning of the work as a whole. Perhaps it was because he did rather see it this way that Bradley found Gloucester a character neither very interesting nor very distinct. Nevertheless, he seems to me both – and of major importance as well – though as always we need to look for 'character' beyond ethical qualities and self-conscious decisions. Edmund and Gloucester are juxtaposed in a rather different way from Lear and Cordelia: Edmund's kind of strength is the complement of his father's kind of weakness, and each makes its comment on the other; yet they are related, as Lear and Cordelia are, in point of need and vulnerability.

Where Edmund is all (or nearly all) hard, contemptuous, masterful ego, Gloucester is wavering, uncertain, fearful, and confused. At bottom, he is a much more various personality than Edmund or Kent, because far more open to experience. But he is obviously so afraid of what might happen to him, so little confident of his own vitality, so unable, for all his air of jocular complacency (about how he got Edmund) in the first scene, to rest secure in his ego, that he would indeed 'unstate [himself] to be in a due resolution' (I, ii, 102–3). He eventually does unstate himself, of course, in one way or another (both good and bad) several times over.

The contradiction of Gloucester's 'tender and entire' love for Edgar being so ready to believe the worst of him is very obvious; so is the way he can proclaim 'I never got him' (meaning that he *did*) and in the storm-scene complain that 'our flesh and blood . . . is grown so vile/That it doth hate what gets it' (meaning that it makes *him* hate *it*). As with Lear, his desire for 'justice' on Edgar is so savage and extreme that it clearly betrays the open wound underneath it. We certainly do not have to wait until the storm-scene to realize his love for him – 'No father his son dearer' (III, iv, 173). The point is not so much Gloucester's confusion or weakness of mind as his helplessness every time in the face of his deepest feelings. Although these, as we see all through, are the best part of him, they leave him feeling too open, too exposed to possible pain, to let himself dare be shaped and confirmed by them. And yet he hankers for the integrity, the fullness, they could give.

It is much too crude to see Gloucester in the sort of terms Edgar uses in Act v – as a man whose vice, lechery, somehow brings moral retribution upon him, like a dose of well-earned moral syphilis, to blind him and open his eyes to the truth. Critics who can see it in that way can obviously learn nothing from Shakespeare about human nature, morality, or even ordinary decency. That the play associates Gloucester's lechery with fire is obvious enough – 'enter Gloucester, with a torch' and so on, in the storm-scene; nevertheless, if the torch he carries into the hovel is a moral emblem, it is also a symbol of light and warmth and comfort, and a gesture of human feeling. In fact, a good deal of the imagery of light and fire in the play centres on Gloucester, but not simply to decorate an essentially crude, moralistic point about him. Rather, it is a medium in which his specific, complex moral being is partly realized: he is characteristically one who fears the darkness of night, who needs light or fire not only to see by, but as a reassuring witness of life itself. The first words he utters after he is blinded make that connection as significantly as the torch he brings to Lear in the hovel:

> All dark and comfortless. Where's my son Edmund?
> Edmund, enkindle all the sparks of nature
> To quit this horrid act.　　　　　(III, vii, 84–6)

The play consistently suggests the inner need that makes him (as it were) play with fire. Nothing marks the difference between him and Lear so much as their first instinctive reactions to the Duke of Cornwall:

> GLOS.　　　　　My dear Lord,
> 　You know the fiery quality of the Duke;
> 　How unremovable and fix'd he is
> 　In his own course.
> LEAR . . . Fiery! what quality?
> 　　　. . . My breath and blood!
> Fiery! the fiery Duke! Tell the hot Duke that –
> 　　　　　　　　　　　　(II, iv, 91ff)

It is not simply that, as Alfred Harbage puts it, Gloucester's 'instinct is to retreat'.[1] It is rather that he is both fascinated by 'fire', and yet shrinks from it out of some half-felt deficiency of it in himself, as though he fears it as much as he wants it. If he is not simply a lecher, one who has had too much 'fire' in the past, neither is he simply a weak man who lacks it altogether. If he had enough to beget Edmund, he also has enough to come to Lear's relief even 'if I die for it, as no less is threatened me', and enough to confront the

---

[1] Alfred Harbage, Introduction to his Pelican ed. of *King Lear*, reprinted in the collection of essays on *Shakespeare: The Tragedies*, which he edited in the Twentieth Century Views Series (New York, 1964), p. 120.

fiery Duke eventually. His 'weakness', his lack of 'fixity', is more an incapacity to expose the whole of himself to life, from a fear that he could not sustain the full experience either of 'fire' or of 'hell-black night'. Yet the mere thought of Lear facing the latter is so unbearable that it brings Gloucester to one due resolution and then another (III, iii and vii, 55ff). We might regard the hell-black cruelty he meets, precipitated by one son, as the nemesis of his credulity and moral vice; all the same, to call the gods 'just' to plague him, as Edgar does, is either to have a pretty nasty conception of justice or a strong need to shuffle something off one's own conscience. For Gloucester's fate extends beyond the blinding to an end precipitated by his other son, by Edgar himself – an end that we might want to see as a more subtle nemesis perhaps, but which is also more poignant and more significant than that.

In the blinding scene Gloucester's strength derives from his utter helplessness. The man who anxiously scrutinized omens and the stars, who has feared what life might bring, now finds it exactly what he had always half-expected it was and himself fully as vulnerable to it as he had always feared. But now he does not have to retreat from it, since there is nowhere to retreat to: 'I am tied to th'stake and I must stand the course'. And so must we – which is surely the crucial dramatic point of the blinding scene. Even leaving the gods out of it, *this* is what the 'hearts' of men and women are capable of: the cold brutality and the sadistic pleasure behind Cornwall and Regan's insistence on 'justice' declare both the point to which no justice or love of justice could be supported, and yet precisely the kind of deed we want justice for. The sheer fact of the blinding, and our sheer horrified rejection of it as unendurable, lie at the very centre of the play. Having endured that, however,

Gloucester also has to suffer the other consequence of his weakness:

> O my follies! Then Edgar was abus'd.
> Kind Gods, forgive me that, and prosper him! (*ibid.*, 90–1)

The word 'prosper' recurs several times in the play, and it always gets ironic handling. Here, not the least of the ironies is that the only real prosperity Edgar will receive from the kind gods is some forgiveness for Gloucester – and Edgar eventually receives it not from the gods but by forcing Gloucester to forgive himself. For at this moment Gloucester surely calls the gods 'kind' more in hope or prayer than in assertion: 'do this and you will (after all) prove kind'. Actually to see them as active in kindness he would have to *be* like that himself (if a man could 'forget and forgive' in the circumstances); but although he has had to endure so much, he has had to do so only passively, as a victim. Characteristically, when he confronts the passionate guilt he has to feel as a responsible agent, his impulse is not active in that sense at all; it is rather to withdraw from the fullness of feeling again into another kind of passivity – the only withdrawal left to him being an inward one. Thus he 'has no way', man is a 'worm', men are 'as flies to wanton boys', the heavens have 'humbled [him] to all strokes'. All he can see to do is to give away first his purse (distributive justice to obey the overwhelming power of the heavens) and then, as a gesture of the same sort, his very self:

> O you mighty Gods!
> This world I do renounce, and in your sights
> Shake patiently my great affliction off;
> If I could bear it longer, and not fall
> To quarrel with your great opposeless wills,
> My snuff and loathed part of nature should
> Burn itself out. If Edgar live, O, bless him! (IV, vi, 34–40)

In short, he sees the gods as 'great opposeless wills' very much as he saw the 'fiery Duke', whose disposition 'all the world well knows, / Will not be rubb'd nor stopp'd' (II, ii, 153-4). And standing, as he thinks, so high above the 'murmuring surge' that it cannot be heard (as if he were above all the power, chances, and potentialities of life itself), he 'renounces' the world and with it the 'I' that cannot bear to experience it any more – the 'I' which, in his pain and despair and self-deluding detachment, he cannot realize is also the very capacity of that world to love and so to 'bless' Edgar.

What Edgar tries to teach him in tricking him out of suicide (IV, vi) – that his 'life's a miracle', that he should think 'the clearest Gods, who make them honours / Of men's impossibilities, have preserved thee' from the 'fiend', and that he must 'bear free and patient thoughts' – is really too much (though it may seem on closer inspection really too little) for Gloucester to absorb. Certainly, when the savagely insane Lear promptly appears, Gloucester can see him still only through the eyes of his own characteristic fears: 'This great world / Shall so wear out to naught' (IV, vi, 136-7). Lear is obviously not 'naught'; mad as he is, he is still very much alive, as is the world he sees around him even here. But for Gloucester, stronger than any fleeting trust in the 'ever-gentle Gods' (IV, vi, 218-20) is the urge to move away from a world he still cannot really bear to experience – indeed, once again to obliterate his very capacity to experience. Having always been driven to want to *know*, because always suspecting the worst, he now finds that all he knows is Lear's suffering and his own, and especially the suffering of the very knowledge he has been driven to:

> . . . how stiff is my vile sense
> That I stand up, and have ingenious feeling
> Of my huge sorrows! Better I were distract:
> So should my thoughts be sever'd from my griefs,
> And woes by wrong imaginations lose
> The knowledge of themselves. (*ibid.*, 281–6)

For all his ostensible fear of quarrelling with the great opposeless wills of the gods, Gloucester has never really had much capacity to sustain that sort of quarrel (those wills are not 'opposeless' to him for nothing). His innermost fear, in fact, has been to sustain that sort of quarrel in himself, for he has always tended to veer from one part of himself to another – the need to be 'fix'd' and to act, like his need to love, always having to fight the need to protect himself from the full brunt of either feeling or decision. Edgar's famous remark about 'ripeness' being all seems the only appropriate answer to a man like Gloucester:

> EDG. Away, old man! give me thy hand: away!
>   King Lear hath lost, he and his daughters ta'en.
>   Give me thy hand; come on.
> GLOU. No further, sir; a man may rot even here.
> EDG. What! in ill thoughts again! Men must endure
>   Their going hence, even as their coming hither:
>   Ripeness is all. Come on.
> GLOU.   And that's true too. (v, ii, 5–11)

And yet if nothing else did, Gloucester's ready acceptance here (like his ambiguous prayer in IV, vi, 218–20) might make us wonder if Edgar's aphorism amounts to much more than a way of fastening one's moral seat-belt before settling back into a kind of passive fatalism. True, Gloucester has not now or ever lived to his full 'natural' limit; it is equally true that no one can say for sure that he has reached it while he *can* 'come on'. But then neither can anyone know for sure the limit of another man's particular nature. Ripeness in men is not the same as in fruit. Of course no one would judge Edgar wrong in saving Gloucester from suicide or making him go on after Lear's defeat; his love does aid and fortify. But on whose journey is he taking him? What end does he aid and fortify Gloucester *for*? The final irony – which must be set hard against 'ripeness is all' as against our own judgments of Gloucester – is that Gloucester's deepest fear of life, his fear of his own vulnerability, is shown by Edgar's doing to have probably been justified all along. He has had to endure so much already, that the moment his 'heart' is brought by Edgar to feel with full, passionate intensity, he shatters.

> EDG.   . . . List a brief tale;
> And when 'tis told, O! that my heart would burst!
>   . . . O! our lives' sweetness,
> That we the pain of death would hourly die
> Rather than die at once! . . .
> [I] never – O fault! – reveal'd myself unto him, . . .
> I ask'd his blessing, and from first to last
> Told him my pilgrimage: but his flaw'd heart,
> Alack, too weak the conflict to support!
> 'Twixt two extremes of passion, joy and grief,
> Burst smilingly.   (v, iii, 181ff)

As a whole, this speech has a clumsy, over-pitched quality, which might perhaps be put down to a well-deserved attack of spiritual jitters in Edgar (though that does not wholly excuse it, I think);[1] but it does underline

---

[1] As has often been pointed out, a good deal of the writing elsewhere in Act v before Cordelia's death is (to say the least) not Shakespeare at his best. It is neither imaginatively intense nor even very attentive; and although it may be dramatically necessary that, while we are being prepared for the final catastrophe, we are not prematurely overawed by anything before it, it does rather look as if Shakespeare's own attention

the relevant points, even if rather unsubtly. So dominated has Edgar been by his own concerns and needs (including the need to give) that he has failed to measure what his father's heart – 'flaw'd' in its way, no doubt, like everybody's – could take; and a sense in Edgar of his own 'flaw' (but not a very profound sense, one must add) puts a rather different light for him on the wish to die and the conditions of going on. 'Burst smilingly', he says; but we can hardly help asking if this is what 'ripeness' really means (just as Gloucester had always feared it did) and how much his 'smile' is not just the sheer relief of dying.

To me the play seems inconceivable without the figure of Gloucester in it – not because he is so important to the plot (which could have been managed easily enough without his specific character being what it is), nor because his experience parallels and so generalizes Lear's (for the more we consider it the less it does quite that), but because his specific character and experience, each subtly shaping the other, realize an aspect of life necessary to give substance to those embodied in the other characters' – especially Edgar's and Lear's. It is most unforgettably realized in his blinding of course, the physical and moral pain of which he cannot evade but cannot bear either, and which is necessary to the action just because we too can neither evade nor readily bear the horror of what is done to him and why. But this is only the extreme moment of what is continually brought home to us by the delicate balance of justice and compassion with which Shakespeare portrays Gloucester's case – a

was so intent on the final scene that he did not bother very much with what had to be spelled out first, especially as it had to fulfil our largely conventional expectations. Still, I do not think we need make too much of it. When the catastrophe does fall, it overwhelms any sense we have of slackness or coasting earlier. In the end, I doubt if the play leaves us with an uncomfortably vivid memory of Shakespeare having nodded.

balance that leaves us no way of separating those qualities. Moralism is as inadequate to Gloucester as mere pity; we are forced to respond with him in sympathetic recognition, and yet also respond against him. For what his case exhibits is the world's power really to hurt – the opaque, irreducible, brutal actuality of what people can do and suffer. It exhibits this as much in what he himself threatens to Edgar, in the blind panic of his own hurt and fear, as in what he suffers from the blind, brutal violence of others – or even from the blindly heedless love of Edgar. The first of these obviously does parallel what Lear does to Cordelia, but as always the similarity only highlights the crucial difference. If the two men are alike in a vulnerability neither can acknowledge in himself, Lear thinks 'nature', reality, is to be commanded where Gloucester fears and mistrusts it. Gloucester's very mistrust, the very recessiveness of his will, makes the lurking savagery he both exhibits and meets in the world seem not only more vividly, more objectively real to us, but also, no matter how much men try to avoid it, utterly inescapable. Just because it can be so harsh and is so unavoidable, indeed, it becomes a measure of Edgar's attempts to master life 'philosophically'; and it pervades our view of Lear's more mental experience too, though more ambiguously – suggesting on the one hand a degree of possible, self-induced illusion in it, but at the same time the potentiality of the world to match the pain and nightmare terrors in Lear's consciousness with appalling physical pain and terror. The blinding scene, for example, represents not so much 'the real thing', as Mr Mason has put it, in contrast to the mere 'play-acting' of Lear and the others in the storm-scenes, as a different but necessary kind of reality – one clearly related to what the characters in the storm suffer mentally, but whose stark, basic, simple physicality *we* can hardly bear.[1] Conversely, their suffering, and everything they are conscious of in those scenes, generalizes the significance of Gloucester's experience, making it for us much more than a casual brutality he just happens to suffer, or merely the result of a particular weakness of character in him. Without Gloucester in the play, the attitudes and behaviour not just of Edmund, Goneril, Regan and Cornwall, but of others too, would seem less serious, less meaningful. It might have seemed, for instance, that there was nothing for Lear to get so worked up about in Goneril and Regan's attitude over the knights, or that his madness is a merely pathological condition. Equally, Lear's state underlines both Gloucester's deep-seated passivity and yet the necessary kind of strength he finds in it. In short, if Lear serves to generalize Gloucester's experience, Gloucester serves to give Lear's a vital reference-point in fact: 'nature', we see, will always give good cause for fear and grief. In relation to Edgar it works rather the other way. Since what Gloucester most fears in life, and in himself, really is to be feared, his case holds before us the possibility that 'losses' – real losses and not simply the idea of losses – finally have no 'remedies'.

IV

This applies especially in the second half of the play. In the first half, the Fool has an analogous (though simpler) role in the action: to insist on the sharp reality of Lear's losses. The Fool's pathos is partly visible to himself, of course. He clearly knows the 'folly' of feelings like those he himself acts from, compared with the commonsense wisdom of the

[1] H. A. Mason, *Shakespeare's Tragedies of Love*, p. 202. I think Paul J. Alpers much nearer the mark: 'King Lear and the Theory of the "Sight Pattern"', in Brower and Poirier (eds.), *In Defense of Reading*, esp. pp. 138, 144, 146ff.

world. He realizes too that his actual behaviour, as well as bringing some comfort to Lear, also reproaches him in a way he cannot afford to reproach him in words. He continually reminds Lear that even in the worldly sense he should not have played the game as he did, but since he did play it, he would have been (and could have afforded to have been) wiser to trust to real feelings rather than to words. But for all the pathos of these contradictions – and of his helplessness – it is important not to sentimentalize the Fool any more than Cordelia. He is limited by what he cannot understand about Lear – how hard a man who *is* able to expect justice can stick by his right to get it. The Fool is limited, that is, as George Orwell and others have pointed out, to a kind of folk-wisdom, which sees the world very sharply and shrewdly, recognizes basic human realities – realities that include basic human feelings – for what they are, but which, it must also be said, always sees the world as it were from below. The Fool cannot expect justice; indeed, he is clear-eyed about so much of life just because he cannot afford the luxury of demanding more.

> Fathers that wear rags
>   Do make their children blind,
> But fathers that bear bags
>   Shall see their children kind.
> Fortune, that arrant whore,
>   Ne'er turns the key to th' poor.
> But for all this thou shalt have as many dolours
> for thy daughters as thou canst tell in a year.   (II, iv, 48–55)

For the Fool, facts and ideals are always and always will be at odds in 'the realm of Albion' (III, ii, 79ff); men always think themselves badly treated by fate; never able simply to accept their own image, even the fortunate will distort themselves out of sheer vanity: 'there was never yet fair woman but she made mouths in a glass' (*ibid.*, 35–6). Folly is the universal condition, and truth 'a dog must to kennel', only to be risked in wary jesting.

The Fool's attitude is not a wholly negative or helpless one, however. While he does tend, as John Danby has remarked, to see man like himself as 'a poor, cowering, threatened creature' who has 'to look after himself as best he can', there is more to him, and thus to his view of man, than that. He is not quite 'helplessly immobilized by a handy-dandy of opposites neither of which he can choose'.[1] Like everyone else in the play, he does choose, even if, like everyone else again, he chooses as he does because (in one sense or another) he has to. The total effect of what he says and what he is, qualifying each other as they do, is not to expose his 'handy-dandy' vision of life as simple 'moral bankruptcy' or 'moral panic'. That vision is rather the condition of the world to which, as *he* sees it, he has to answer with such resources of vitality and spirit as he has; and as *we* see it, part of his answer is indeed to see the world like that. For him, the basic human realities have simply to be accepted and borne, though men make a wry mouth in doing so. Nevertheless, it is essentially a deflationary view, unable to rise to the highest demands on life, but equally incapable of illusion about it; and his role is to push this view at Lear with an insistence that, if it does not help drive him mad, does not exactly help to keep him sane either.

In other words, like the other minor characters, the Fool is a figure who both comments on Lear and is commented upon. The 'reality' he sees and the human qualities prompting and answering to that view of things – the 'foolish' loyalty, the violence, the wry, deflationary humour – while they afford Lear some comfort, also continually

[1] John F. Danby, *Shakespeare's Doctrine of Nature* (London, 1949), pp. 108ff.

underscore (even to Lear's own reluctant consciousness) the simple fact of what Lear has done and the possibility that he did it out of some failure in himself. They continually force him back against the pain less of guilt, I think, than of loss – an intimation of some profound insecurity in himself that he cannot acknowledge. So, although the Fool's sense of reality, clear-eyed and humane as it is, could be liberating, it would be so only if its limitations did not matter. And they do. Its strength is very vividly realized in the storm-scenes, for example:

LEAR Arraign her first; 'tis Goneril. I here take my oath before this honourable assembly, she kick'd the poor King her father.
FOOL Come hither, mistress. Is your name Goneril?
LEAR She cannot deny it.
FOOL Cry you mercy, I took you for a joint-stool. (III, vi, 47ff)

This comes like a breath of freedom from the grip of Lear's insane fantasy. And yet, in releasing us for a moment into the daylight of common reality, it is powerless to do more, since Lear's grotesque vision is not merely insane. It answers to an aspect of life that the Fool simply cannot. Significantly enough, the storm-scenes realize equally vividly both the Fool's strength and the limits of what it can meet. Once things reach this pass, they have clearly gone beyond any wryly adaptive acceptance of life such as his. That side of his role in the action is subsumed, as it were, in Gloucester's, and (perhaps because of this) he disappears from sight.

V

That we cannot accept either the Fool's or Gloucester's essential passivity as adequate responses to life is obvious enough, but, as I suggested earlier, it seems to me a fact crucial to the action as a whole. Such attitudes almost irresistibly provoke *us* toward action – even if it is only the action of the mind in judging what, as we see it, ultimately victimizes them. Their 'losses' prompt us to look for 'remedies' – that is, to seek 'justice' – even if we seek it in a more inclusive view of what life may be. In short, our desire for justice also springs from our sense of some insult to human weakness, insecurity, vulnerability, our own or another's, that we cannot bear to accept – though that of course in turn prompts the question whether what we are seeking is more than some way of bearing our own vulnerability, and a way that we perhaps have to find – or rather, make – for ourselves.

To evoke something like these considerations with inescapable force is the chief function of the scene between Goneril and Albany (IV, ii), giving it in fact a quite pivotal place in the action. It comments on nearly every human act in the play – not just those in the blinding scene that immediately precedes it, but also Lear's furious demands on Cordelia or his other daughters for 'justice', or Gloucester's demands on Edgar, or Edmund's demands from 'Nature', Gloucester's decision to help Lear in the storm, Cordelia's return in arms, her 'no cause, no cause', Edgar's killing of Oswald or Lear's of the hangman: every act, in short, prompted by the love, the ineradicable human need, of justice. And just as the role of the servant in the blinding-scene, who dares to oppose 'the fiery Duke' and actually kills him, is simply to speak and act as he unforgettably does on that one occasion, so it is almost Albany's chief function in the play to be the centre of the subsequent scene with Goneril.

As we instinctively move *with* the servant in the blinding-scene, even though the immediate results of his act are only his own death as well as the Duke's and the loss of Gloucester's other eye, so we move in this scene with

Albany. The opening dialogue between Goneril and Edmund reminds us that for them the venturesome daring of their spirits (no matter what the cost to others) marks their superiority to such as Albany and

> the cowish terror of his spirit
> That dares not undertake; he'll not feel wrongs
> Which tie him to an answer. (IV, ii, 12–14)

Albany's opening remark to Goneril seems to bear them out: he 'fears her disposition'. He sees that disposition in essentially moral terms, to be valued in organic relation to a 'Nature' that is itself organically normative. His voice seems that of a rather commonplace man perhaps, but basically sane, moral, slow and over-cautious no doubt ('self-reproving', Edmund calls him), but finally outraged by what he sees – a kind of decently worried Elizabethan Humanist:

> That nature, which contemns its origin,
> Cannot be border'd certain in itself;
> She that herself will sliver and disbranch
> From her material sap, perforce must wither
> And come to deadly use.
> GON. No more; the text is foolish.
> ALB. Wisdom and goodness to the vile seem vile;
> Filths savour but themselves. What have you done?
> Tigers, not daughters, what have you perform'd?
> A father, and a gracious aged man,
> Whose reverence even the head-lugg'd bear would lick,
> Most barbarous, most degenerate! have you madded.
> Could my good brother suffer you to do it!
> A man, a prince, by him so benefited!
> If that the heavens do not their visible spirits
> Send quickly down to tame these vilde offences,
> It will come,
> Humanity must perforce prey on itself,
> Like monsters of the deep. (32ff)

The imaginative – and hence moral – power of this is clearly impressive in itself; moreover, it is impressively endorsed by the action. We have actually seen, and not only in Goneril and Regan, how one self after another, once divided from its own 'heart', becomes driven by forces within it which it all too readily takes as forces constraining it from outside. We have also seen how its allowing itself to come to such 'use' is indeed a self-withering. Particular dispositions do make their own sense of 'reality': filths do savour but themselves. We may have a passing doubt about Lear as 'a father, and a gracious aged man' (or wonder if a bear would be altogether well-advised to try to lick him); but perhaps a terrifying capacity for violence and wrong-doing to the good seem good. Nevertheless, the coldly willed, self-admiring brutality with which Goneril has used Lear's weakness to 'mad' him even to point of danger, not to mention the business with Edmund, or her attitude to Gloucester (although she was not present at the blinding, it was originally her idea to 'pluck out his eyes' – and the very word, *pluck*, catches her spirit): these are surely barbarous and degenerate enough to place behind Albany's words apparently the whole authority of the play. Yet once again it is not quite the whole.

For one thing, since we know what Albany does not know as yet – Gloucester's 'punishment' and what has happened since that – we can hardly help wondering if humanity has not come to preying on itself already. True, Albany himself shows the kind of human restraint he means:

> Were't my fitness
> To let these hands obey my blood,
> They are apt enough to dislocate and tear
> Thy flesh and bones; howe'er thou are a fiend,
> A woman's shape doth shield thee. (*ibid.*, 63–7)

But even here we feel the impulse of the blood, the material sap, to 'dislocate and tear' as more vividly real (and perhaps a little extreme for what Albany knows her to have done?) than the values implicit in 'fitness' or 'woman' or 'shield'. The point is made still more obvious: when Albany now receives the news of Gloucester's blinding, and of the servant, 'thrill'd with remorse', killing Cornwall, his response is significant for being so wholly natural:

> This shows you are above,
> You justicers, that these our nether crimes
> So speedily can venge! But, O poor Gloucester!
> Lost he his other eye? (*ibid.*, 78–81)

But of course the 'visible spirit' was that within a man, not an external agent as it were dropped from the heavens on a special mission; the 'taming' was no less bloody than the deed to which it brought justice – in fact, the only *taming* that took place was that of Gloucester. Albany's distinction between nature as barbarous and nature as normative – between tigers and daughters, 'material sap' and 'monsters of the deep' – begins to dissolve before our eyes. The murder of Cornwall was as much humanity preying on itself as a spirit intervening from outside it. The bloody impulse to revenge, to turn oneself to the 'use' of *lex talionis*, is not distinguishable in nature from the sap of men's lives, their very capacity to be *thrilled* with 'remorse' (or passionately moved to other impulses) at whatever they cannot endure. The scene ends with Albany an example of life asserting itself in precisely that way – moral sense, active power, even violence, inseparable from each other – and setting off to do a bit of preying on humanity himself:

> Gloucester, I live
> To thank thee for the love thou show'dst the king,
> And to revenge thine eyes. (*ibid.*, 94–6)

VI

As a whole, this fourth Act of *King Lear* seems to me to illustrate Shakespeare's capacity to think about life so powerfully that the energy of the thinking cannot be distinguished from the most powerful capacity to create its object: swiftly, incisively, cumulatively, and in the most searching and disciplined particularity. There is an astonishing and beautiful economy not merely in the way each scene is built, but in the way they are all so tellingly juxtaposed as the action is developed through them. The effect is more substantial than (as at least one critic has suggested) a series of ironic contrasts each of which merely undercuts successive 'affirmations'.[1] It is rather a complex series of considerations, some of which are undoubtedly ironical in that way, but which also gather substance and mutual inter-relationships in our minds as they unfold. A case in point is the relation between the scene with Albany and Goneril and the earlier blinding-scene; another is its relation with the one immediately following, which contains the Gentleman's description of Cordelia – a passage that, brief as it is, becomes a new but necessary element in our whole sense of the action:

> . . . now and then an ample tear trill'd down
> Her delicate cheek; it seem'd she was a queen
> Over her passion; who, most rebel-like,
> Sought to be king o'er her.
> KENT   O! then it mov'd her.
> GENT. Not to a rage; patience and sorrow strove
> Who should express her goodliest. You have seen
> Sunshine and rain at once; her smiles and tears
> Were like, a better way; those happy smilets
> That play'd on her ripe lip seem'd not to know

[1] Brooke, 'The Ending of *King Lear*', in Bloom (ed.), *Shakespeare 1564–1964*.

> What guests were in her eyes; which parted thence,
> As pearls from diamonds dropp'd. In brief,
> Sorrow would be a rarity most belov'd,
> If all could so become it. (IV, iii, 13ff)

I do not believe anyone can think of Cordelia after this speech without thinking of her in terms of it. Its beauty, which has no less imaginative and moral power than Albany's speech about material sap and monsters of the deep, lies in the sense of life it evokes with such feeling. That life consists in an openness to feeling apparently so complete that it becomes a balance of spirit at once miraculous and precariously vulnerable. The conflict of patience and sorrow here trembles just short of the conflict of joy and grief that finally shatters Gloucester; the hair'sbreadth difference between the two is crucial. At the same time, however, it is impossible not to feel something *over-* delicate in this image – something that might perhaps lead us, faced with the rather over-rapturous view of it that many people take, to speak as bluntly as H. A. Mason does about the 'insufferable conceits' of the passage.[1] But if that would be to lean over backwards, the verse surely does (in the 'happy smilets', for example) become rather too sweet, a little caressing, almost (in the strained image of the pearls and diamonds) coming to the verge of a melting dissolution. The touch of weakness does matter dramatically, I think, though it seems to reflect less on what is presented in this view of Cordelia than what is left out of it. What is left out of it is not so much her human failings – the strain of wilful rectitude we saw earlier, for example – as her human need (and capacity) to act at all. This patience and sorrow explicitly avoid 'rage'; she is notably still, an image

[1] Mason, *Shakespeare's Tragedies of Love*, p. 215. Mason is obviously reacting against such views as D. A. Traversi's – e.g. in his *An Approach to Shakespeare*, 2 vols., rev. and expanded (New York, 1969), II, 161ff.

to be contemplated. Nor does 'patience' here suggest that she is now the leader of an army, nor has that aspect of her anything to do with what really moves us. On the contrary, we are moved by the tremulous balance she seems to embody, her very stillness, her inability to *do* anything but only *be* herself; and all the more so because these mark her sharp difference from the world dynamically moved by men's 'rage' and actions. Juxtaposed with Albany, she offers a beautiful – to many people, an overwhelmingly beautiful – image of what human life might be: the image of a 'patience' very different, in its openness to feeling and its power to assimilate it, from his, which is more a simple cautiousness that easily turns turtle under the impact of strong feeling, or from Kent's, which can only fasten itself more tightly in its own safe anchorage, or from Gloucester's, which is only a suppressed panic that eventually lets itself drift towards mere resignation. Cordelia's appearance in the following scene (IV, iv) reinforces the same vision of her. Not only does the 'nature' to which she looks offer valuable 'idle weeds' as well as 'sustaining corn', 'repose' to match 'the eye of anguish', 'secrets' that are 'bless'd', 'virtues' that spring with tears, the power to 'govern' rage. She herself will meet the British 'powers'. Her arms are 'incited' by 'love, dear love'; 'love' is in turn matched with her 'ag'd father's right'. All through, in fact, it is the same vision of a paradoxical, almost impossible, balance – in 'nature', because in her. And what it can effect is realized, with a power almost unbearably moving, in the subsequent reconciliation scene:

LEAR   . . . Do not laugh at me;
    For as I am a man, I think this lady
    To be my child Cordelia.
COR.   And so I am, I am.   (IV, vii, 68–70)

It is easy to understand, therefore, why some critics see Cordelia as an embodiment of 'Christian patience' or, like Edgar, a 'figure of spiritual perfection' (to quote D. G. James),[1] and quite out of place at the head of an army. It is equally understandable that, given this view of her, such perfection would seem to others (Bradley and Granville-Barker, for instance) to carry an inherent 'impotence' with it: it is both her strength and her weakness to be above ordinary life. But to leave it like that is to overlook the crucial similarity between Cordelia's goodness and the attitudes, both good and bad, of the other characters. Despite the ideal possibility she seems to embody here, despite the beauty and value of that possibility, it is not the whole of her, nor does she stand apart from the world of the other characters. Neither can the possibility she represents here. Even at its richest and finest, her outlook cannot, any more than theirs, encompass and hold firmly in its grasp everything it seeks to transmute into its own terms – in her case, the terms of a full and harmonious goodness. To be good, one has to do good; goodness exists only in so far as it remakes bad things and gives them a different meaning, even if only in the way they are seen. True, Cordelia's goodness does partly do that; in fact, it is not 'impotent' at all. She does not lose the battle, for instance, *because* of her goodness. If one sort of pious sentimentality imagines that good is always likely to prevail simply because it is good, it is only another sort to suppose that good proves itself good by not prevailing. Cordelia's is effective enough, as the reconciliation scene, with the power of everything else in the play that flows into it, surely testifies. But the other

---

[1] John F. Danby, '*King Lear* and Christian Patience', in his book, *Poets on Fortune's Hill* (London, 1952); D. G. James, *The Dream of Learning* (Oxford, 1951), pp. 113–14.

side of it is equally visible there too: in what is not quite just in her view of Lear, in her 'no cause, no cause', in the 'rage' that has to be 'killed' in him, and in the final reference to the necessary bloody 'arbitrement' between the powers of the kingdom – a kingdom which, whether the inner kingdom of man or the outward kingdom of the world, is not hers, but always Lear's own. In short, the harmonious balance she seems to represent here is vulnerable to the forces, both from within and from outside, that it must hold together in order to exist at all, but which can no longer hold together the moment it does exist, at least not in any recognizably human terms. For the need to act is also an essential element in human beings, yet no action arises from, nor can it sustain, such a *stasis*. Given what men are, to love justice is inevitably to seek it, and to seek it is inevitably to destroy in the process what Cordelia seems to represent; so far, Bradley and Granville-Barker are right. And yet what she represents is precisely the kind of inner justice, a justice of the 'heart', that answers to the balance that men are impelled to find, or to make, in acting upon the outward world of 'nature' itself.

The action of the play has irresistibly involved us in this process as well, however. In so far as we have also felt what impels Kent, or Edmund, or Gloucester, or Albany, or Lear, or even Cordelia herself at the beginning, we have become part of the same world, the conflicting energies of which necessarily destroy the possibility she has come to represent. Being *that*, how could it survive? The very agitation of our passions, to use Johnson's phrase, which so completely involves us in the current of the poet's imagination – even in our very judging of the people and events, for judging is a form of action – has involved us unwittingly in complicity with the logic by which she is killed by the world of action, conflict, and (what goes with them) mis-chance. The details of how her death actually happens do not in the final analysis matter much, for, although we resist the possibility to the end, it is bound to happen one way or another in 'the common events of human life'. It is a conclusion the very premises of which are subtly laid in the same grounds as our wish – indeed, our active effort – to reject it. That the immediate cause is the conflicting tangle of activity that brings justice to Regan, Goneril, and Edmund is certainly appropriate enough – appropriate precisely because we find that justice so satisfying. Nobody, I notice, has ever felt much compunction about them: if Shakespeare hardly encourages us to think of them at this stage as real human beings any more, that fact might prompt us to wonder how readily we would accept even this little demonstration of moral justice if he had made us do so. Nor, in the flow of the action, do I believe we feel Cordelia any less herself, or any less a 'queen', in resorting to war in support of her father's 'right'. Or to come by an-other route back to an earlier point: even as we start wondering perhaps if the necessary 'arbitrement' with the evil-doers is what we had really wanted, seeing what is lost with Cordelia in the process, we surely still respond with the life left in Lear that judges the hangman a mere 'slave' and kills him.

4

Lear and 'true need'

It is possible to realize what Cordelia is and what she represents only if one can bear to realize it in oneself, and for a
large part of the action Lear himself cannot. The relevant
quality is not Love, however, or an ideal goodness, much
less sanctity; despite the way some critics talk, I doubt if
we should really prefer it even if Lear did emerge from the
reconciliation-scene with a wee halo of redemption over
his head. What Cordelia represents is something necessary
to love or goodness or sanctity no doubt, but certainly not
identical with any of them, for it is no less necessary to any
way of being fully alive. We might call it an open and vital
'patience' or an 'integrity of being', but such abstractions
are hopelessly vague and ambiguous. Indeed, part of the
greatness of the play lies in the sharp subtlety with which
it distinguishes between the meanings that words like
'patience' or 'integrity' can have, and in the power with
which it makes us acknowledge in Cordelia what either
quality might mean at its best – even while making us also
recognize, along with its necessity, its insufficiency in itself.
Yet if we have to recognize that insufficiency even in her,
who embodies it in its purest form, only in the other
characters can its significance and limits be properly explored, and especially in the two who reach out furthest –
Edgar and Lear. The others invoke the gods; these two try
in one way or another to comprehend them, though of

course it is to Lear's experience and consciousness that we are mainly directed.

I

Lear is not merely forced to experience the results of what he willed in the first scene; more terrifyingly, despite every resistance he can discover in himself, he is forced inch by inch to recognize that he *is* being forced to. The will he thought was autonomous turns out not to be autonomous, nor even effective. He is, it emerges, what he had not much admitted to himself – not the absolute master of his world (as kings and babies both tend to assume), but a part of objective reality as other people see it and therefore vulnerable to their wills. What Gloucester, for example, or the Fool had always *assumed* about himself, Lear has to discover; and the shock and the pain of the discovery lie chiefly in his very helplessness to avoid making it. In his very first conflict with Goneril (I, iv), for example, he is clearly enraged by far more than her 'ingratitude' or his own 'folly'. These are only the terms in which he can admit the cause to himself – terms that subtly reassert his own generosity of heart and uncompromised will at the beginning, as if he had been merely led astray by a particular, though quite serious, miscalculation. But his actual behaviour and his most powerful speeches betray a more intractable conflict underneath the obvious one.

For a start, we have to recognize that he faces in Goneril more than a hypocritical ingrate. She is a much more formidable reality than that. Whatever her conscious intentions, her speech evinces a moral outlook that has a quite genuine force in its way:

> This admiration, Sir, is much o' th' savour
> Of other your new pranks. I do beseech you
> To understand my purposes aright:

As you are old and reverend, should be wise.
Here do you keep a hundred knights and squires;
Men so disorder'd, so debosh'd, and bold,
That this our court, infected with their manners,
Shows like a riotous inn: epicurism and lust
Makes it more like a tavern or a brothel
Than a grac'd palace. The shame itself doth speak
For instant remedy; be then desir'd
By her, that else will take the thing she begs,
A little to disquantity your train;
And the remainders, that shall still depend,
To be such men as may besort your age,
Which know themselves and you.

LEAR   Darkness and devils!   (I, iv, 245ff)

The tone, the imagery, the very rhythms of this speech are sharply illuminated by the interchange with her husband towards the end of the same scene:

ALB. Well, you may fear too far.
GON.   Safer than trust too far.
    Let me still take away the harms I fear,
    Not fear still to be taken: I know his heart. (*ibid.*, 338–40)

It is true, of course: she does know Lear's heart – in the only terms in which he has given it to her, but more importantly in the only terms she can know anything: that is, of threats from, and aggression towards, the external world. And in those terms, Lear *is* liable 'to hold our lives in mercy' – as she fears. For the control visible in Goneril's speech is the kind necessary to keep the world at bay, as though she could not cope with her experience of it otherwise; and in seeing the world like that, as Kent's contrasting but equally one-sided attitude to Lear underlines, her attitude is precisely what makes the world to be feared. If Lear gave her justice rather than love, the whole drift of her speech is to lay down the judgments, the role, she not only demands, but in her deepest self really needs Lear to fit. The note of moral revulsion is spontaneous and wholly characteristic. So too are the narrowness of her moral categories and the intensity with which she applies them. The rampant ego can see personal relationships only as power-relationships – as in her view of Lear as merely childish, for example, and more especially in the way she assumes 'pranks' should be treated, as well as in her open threats. There is zest in the way she crisply 'lays it on the line'. The power of her verse lies in the security and freedom achieved by keeping the facts wholly outside herself, and the strict command she can therefore exercise over them within. (She is a more interesting character than Regan, who seems little more than a moral cretin: her own convenience is the only principle, almost the only reality, Regan ever seems much aware of.)

Against Goneril's view of him, Lear unavailingly tries to counterpose a number of alternative views of himself – all of them insisting on the sovereignty of his *subjective* being, his rights, desires, and will. Thus Kent's recognition of the 'authority' in his very countenance was reassuring exactly where he was already a little troubled. If he had felt any 'faint neglect of late' from Goneril he 'will look further into't' (the familiar note of uneasy authority); if the Fool pressed too hard, there was always the whip (as the Fool points out, the Lear family is very ready with that device for putting things straight); and when he finally confronts Goneril herself it seems at first only a matter of re-asserting his conscious identity. Hence his blustering questions:

> Does any here know me? This is not Lear:
> Does Lear walk thus? speak thus? Where are his eyes?
> Either his notion weakens, his discernings
> Are lethargied – Ha! waking? 'tis not so.
> Who is it that can tell me who I am?   (*ibid.*, 234–8)

The Fool's interjection – 'Lear's shadow' – is doubly true, however. The man Goneril insists on addressing is indeed only Lear's shadow, not the active, subjective reality Lear insists he is; but neither, on the other hand, is his inmost reality the sovereign consciousness he insists on while shouting down any self-doubts about it. The conscious 'I' only obscures the other, and perhaps the shadowed reality could answer the question better than the self Lear takes as real.

> . . . by the marks of sovereignty, knowledge, and reason,
> I should be false persuaded I had daughters. (*ibid.*, 240–2)

This, like the whole view of reality implicit in it, is no more true (though no less true) an image of himself than that implicit in Goneril's reply: 'As you are old and reverend, should be wise'. If his own nature, like Nature at large, offers his consciousness a norm like 'reason', it offers another like 'wisdom'; but in fact it offers very different possibilities as well: 'darkness and devils', 'marble-hearted fiend', 'sea-monster', 'detested kite'. Lear's 'disclaiming' of Cordelia at the beginning showed an appalling violence; but that is far outdone by the positively destructive savagery of his curses on Goneril. His verse 'realizes' the external, natural correlatives of what in his self is also made visibly real to us, though not to him: an energy that can be made barren and tormented by a kind of self-frustration, an urge to command all forms of life so fierce that it virtually becomes a will to prey on them.

> Hear, Nature, hear! dear Goddess, hear! . . .
> Into her womb convey sterility! . . .
> And from her derogate body never spring
> A babe to honour her! If she must teem,
> Create her child of spleen, that it may live
> And be a thwart disnatur'd torment to her!

Let it stamp wrinkles in her brow of youth,
With cadent tears fret channels in her cheeks. . . .

(ibid., 284ff)

The highly active verbs here are characteristic of Lear. He always apprehends nature as dynamic, in action; part of his greatness is to perceive, to inhabit as his own, a world always in awe-inspiring movement. Being a world of energies, it is a world inevitably in conflict. When he apprehends it differently – as a frame of order, for instance, as when he refers to the 'most small fault' in Cordelia that 'wrench'd my frame of nature / From the fix'd place' (*ibid.*, 277–8) – it is significantly unconvincing. The violence of 'wrench'd' betrays the self-protective conception of himself implicit in 'fix'd place' – as if anyone's nature, let alone his in particular, ever had such a thing, or as if his behaviour had been a simple matter of letting 'thy folly in / And thy dear judgment out'. But as with 'patience', there are different meanings for words like 'energy' and 'conflict'. For example, both in this scene with Goneril and later on in the reconciliation scene Lear is moved to tears – the passive verb is exactly appropriate. Nevertheless, the 'wheel' he later feels bound to seems to move, the 'fire' to be alive, and tears to 'scald like molten lead' – all with a kind of energy very different from any he apprehends here in confronting Goneril. Both are painful; in one way, the present kind may strike us as even more active; and yet it is as diffused and distracted as he is:

>   . . . Life and death! I am asham'd
> That thou hast power to shake my manhood thus,
> That these hot tears, which break from me perforce,
> Should make thee worth them. Blasts and fogs upon thee!
> Th'untented woundings of a father's curse
> Pierce every sense about thee! Old fond eyes,

Beweep this cause again, I'll pluck ye out,
And cast you, with the waters that you loose,
To temper clay. Yea, is't come to this?
Ha! Let it be so: I have another daughter,
Who, I am sure, is kind and comfortable:
When she shall hear this of thee, with her nails
She'll flay thy wolvish visage. Thou shalt find
That I'll resume the shape which thou dost think
I have cast off for ever.   (*ibid.*, 305-19)

This is a form of energy ('shake', 'blasts', 'pierce', 'pluck', 'cast', 'flay', and so on) answering to the violent effort of Lear's will to hold together a consciousness of his manhood, fatherhood, and power – a familiar shape or identity, whose authority lies in the abstract roles it assumes. It is so badly shaken not because it is denied, but because its hidden premiss – the helpless emotional need it is designed to cover – has once again been implicitly but undeniably made visible, more so indeed by Goneril, who pushes his help-lessness at him, than by Cordelia, who pushed at him the arbitrariness of his demands. Again he can only somehow *will* an answering 'justice' from the world; but his will is now compromised by meeting the hard reality of another will that he cannot simply banish from his world. He is moved 'perforce' to tears, which expose the very nakedness, the untented wounds, he cannot bear to acknowledge. All he can do is attempt to deny the reality of the tears. And since his 'energy' is generated from holding his will both against his capacity to feel and against acknowledging that capacity as part of himself (his 'heart' in fact, which makes him as vulnerable, helpless, and demanding as a 'babe'), he inevitably twists wildly towards thoughts of plucking out his own eyes. Nor is that idea a mere fantasy of what the energies of nature, whether in 'darkness and devils' or in animals or in humans, can actually perform – as we eventually witness. Indeed, we are made to see the human impulse to do such things as born from the same need as Lear reveals here. Again and again in the play, action derives from the individual's not being able simply and patiently to accept his own or others' vulnerability to feeling. We do not need the mad Lear to suggest the kinship between the love of justice and the love of cruelty. Both 'loves' are clearly fascinated and made restless by other people's vulnerability, the one to compensate it, the other to exploit it; and both repeatedly manifest the individual's inability to endure his own vulnerability except by masking it from himself, or trying to neutralize it in action upon the external world, or both. It is almost as if the whole of life, natural and human, could realize itself fully only by preying on itself – not in any Darwinian sense of course, but in that every form of 'justice' willed by either men or 'the gods' imposes an order on reality that at once fulfils and diminishes it, and does so both outside us and within us.

But this possibility emerges only as the action unfolds, culminating not just in Cordelia's death but in Lear's (and our own) plight beyond that. Here, throughout the first two acts, we are still with Lear – a Lear still trying more and more desperately to keep the pieces of his acknowledgeable identity together. By the time he confronts Regan, and then both daughters together (II, iv), it is visibly only a threadbare patchwork, and his will clearly attempting the impossible. Against their merciless stripping of every last shred of external 'authority' with which he might identify himself, he seeks indulgence in the name of natural duty, comfort in the name of natural gratitude, protection from pain as just payment for goods received. Flattering one moment and threatening the next, he tries to seize upon a world of powerful 'vengeances of Heaven' – 'nimble lightnings' and 'blinding flames' – because Goneril's eyes 'burn' him; upon another world of natural 'offices' and 'bonds' because he wants to constrain Regan to provide the 'comfort' that will keep his ego in one piece; and upon another world again of an elemental struggle for survival, of wolf and owl and 'necessity's sharp pinch', because he senses what is really at stake for that ego.

And yet we may well wonder why the possibility of madness had already occurred to him immediately after the earlier quarrel with Goneril. 'O! let me not be mad, not mad, sweet heaven' (I, v, 47): is it the thought of having done Cordelia wrong? or the thought that his whole moral calculus has been hopelessly awry? or perhaps the fear that he cannot hide from reality in any other way? Or is he also moved towards madness by what we can see is a more positive and vital impulse – actually to *become* the self-conflicting and thus helplessly vulnerable reality his conscious will refuses to acknowledge? (If that idea about madness seems to belong too much to our own age, it does not necessarily follow that, because earlier times lacked our intellectual advantages, everyone then was blind to the realities of human experience.) Certainly, Lear's climactic act of will is highly ambivalent:

> O! reason not the need . . .
> Allow not nature more than nature needs,
> Man's life is cheap as beast's . . .
>   But, for true need,—
> You Heavens, give me that patience, patience I need!—
> You see me here, you Gods, a poor old man,
> As full of grief as age; wretched in both! . . .
>   . . . fool me not so much
> To bear it tamely; touch me with noble anger,
> And let not women's weapons, water-drops,
> Stain my man's cheeks! No, you unnatural hags,

I will have such revenges on you both
That all the world shall – I will do such things,
What they are, yet I know not, but they shall be
The terrors of the earth. You think I'll weep;
No, I'll not weep:
I have full cause of weeping, but this heart
Shall break into a hundred thousand flaws
Or ere I'll weep. O Fool! I shall go mad.   (II, iv, 266ff)

This – both in the spectacle Lear exhibits and in the considerations his speech evokes – precipitates a great deal
that has been accumulating in our minds during the first
two Acts, and pushes it irresistibly onwards towards the
third Act. On the one side, obviously, the only way Lear's
will can keep itself and so his familiar identity intact is 'to
abjure all roofs, and choose / To wage against th'enmity o'
th' air', as he put it a little earlier (210–11): to choose his
own conditions, however extreme, rather than suffer
others'. Thus he both flings himself out of human society
(if this castle can be said to represent it), and is forced out.
The two women know what they are about, of course, and
if they don't they should. Equally, though, whatever Lear
means by the remark, they clearly do embody in the external world a disease that is very much in his flesh within.
His speech about 'need' significantly breaks off when it
brings him face to face with the utter impotence of his will
to *make* the external world yield satisfaction. His threats of
'revenge' are like a child's, at once absurd and pathetic in
their grotesque vagueness. His effort to deny not just his
tears but his very capacity to weep – his effort to see it only
as lack of power, and the tears only as a poor kind of wea-
pon – testifies to a reality he can now barely *not* acknowledge.

On the other side, however, his speech also breaks off at
an even more significant point: 'But, for true need—'. He is
clearly right in insisting on the difference between man and

beast, life and mere existence. Human nature does need more. But why? Is it simply because men *want* more? And what do they want precisely? Lear breaks off as if he cannot or will not follow the idea through. If it is only that he arbitrarily wants more, it would be embarrassing enough to admit it so openly; yet it is even more impossible for him to acknowledge that what he cannot name as 'true need' is what, of necessity, he has had to want all along, even (or rather, especially) from Cordelia.

Lear is really caught in a double contradiction. He needs others to respect his external 'authority', the 'marks' of his familiar self, all the qualities indeed with which he can readily identify himself just because they are respected. He needs others' respect in order to respect himself. Yet once again the very urgency of this need betrays the fear behind it – which is a form not of self-ignorance, but rather of self-mistrust, as if he cannot believe, fully, securely and patiently believe, in his mere self as *worth* the love and respect it needs. From the very beginning, as we have seen, he has wanted to believe he is worth them; but while he has always wanted respect and love to be given him freely, 'superfluously', he has also demanded them as moral repayments, given because he 'ought' to have them. The contradiction is no less acute with Goneril and Regan than it was with Cordelia, even though he is clearly not so foolish as to expect these two to give him love. He can and does only expect, out of mere justice, a respect *freely* given yet nevertheless *owed* him for what he gave; and the fact that he gave them more a kind of justice than the love he would have liked it to appear, does not make him any the less conscious that he gave it freely and deserves no less himself.

Beneath that contradiction, however, lies what he can never acknowledge to them or even fully to himself: a desperate hollowness at the heart of his own sense of himself, which could be filled only by a respect and a love given him for no 'reason' or 'cause'. Only these could reassure him that his mere self was real and worthy – real and worthy enough, in fact, for its weakness to be acknowledged by himself because acknowledged by others. Thus, paradoxically, were that need satisfied he could then quite justly claim as owed to him what he now needs. In short, he is caught in a whirligig of need; and all his consciousness can do is reach out for a false image of his 'true need': for 'patience' and the power to execute 'revenge'.

What Lear means by patience here is not much more than the ability to hold his 'tough sides' together, to endure others' denial of his need by a willed denial that they touch his real self. Nor can he allow himself more than a false sense of his pain:

> You see me here, you Gods, a poor old man,
> As full of grief as age . . .

This grief is much too conscious of itself to be what he claims for it – the full state of his mind. Clearly, the self-pity is another self-protective device of his ego, and the gods a paper-audience. But while it would be a mistake, however tempting, to see him and his daughters in his own terms, we *are* surely moved to compassion with him, though for significantly different reasons. For he is pitiful precisely in being reduced to self-pity. Much the same applies in the immediate counter-movement of his mind, from self-pity to the plea, '[you Gods] fool me not so much / To bear it tamely'. The words he uses – not just 'patience', but also 'noble anger' – do afford a glimpse of his true needs: the nature and bearing of which have now to be explored in the storm-scenes and beyond. For if Regan (who has a gift for the convenient truism) is right enough, and

> to wilful men,
> The injuries that they themselves procure
> Must be their schoolmasters,   (*ibid.*, 304-6)

such rightness is merely disgusting in her mouth, nor is it
any more adequate to the truth than Edgar's 'the gods are
just, and of our pleasant vices / Make instruments to
plague us'. Obviously, the desire for 'noble anger' is badly
compromised in Lear as we see him at this point – the impulse to hit back acknowledging no limit because unable to
acknowledge its real cause. But the energy, the power, that
does not bear such treatment 'tamely' is surely a human
need too. These two daughters are indeed 'unnatural hags',
even if not quite for the reasons he thinks they are;
'revenges', if not quite in his terms, are what they call for;
'anger', though not his largely self-baffled fury, would be
'noble'. Both sides partly are in the wrong, and ironically
enough for related reasons; but of course that does not put
them equally in the right.

II

The storm-scenes of Act III bring Lear and Edgar together
for the first time. Each has been reduced to rock-bottom
necessity; each, moreover, forms a kind of commentary on
the other. Both of them have chosen to abjure the social
world and to wage with the enmity of the air itself; and
although the decision is significantly different in each, it is
also significantly alike. Lear's is the unreflective movement
of rage – the only way his will can still realize its power.
Edgar on the other hand is a true member of the Gloucester family, all of whom in one way or another seem
insecure and anxious about themselves, and whose characteristic psychic style is defensive beside the bolder, more

challenging, self-confidently active style characteristic of the Lear family. Edgar's decision – it is his first major speech, incidentally, and obviously invites comparison with his brother's first major speech in Act I, scene ii – is quite deliberately taken in order to defend himself:

> Whiles I may 'scape,
> I will preserve myself; and am bethought
> To take the basest and most poorest shape
> That ever penury, in contempt of man,
> Brought near to beast; my face I'll grime with filth,
> Blanket my loins, elf all my hair in knots,
> And with presented nakedness outface
> The winds and persecutions of the sky . . .
> . . . Poor Turlygod! poor Tom!
> That's something yet: Edgar I nothing am.   (II, iii, 5ff)

Like Lear, he has little option; but it is worth noticing in the first place the keynote of his behaviour and attitudes throughout the action given us here explicitly at the beginning: 'I will preserve myself'. If the touch of complacency many critics have noted in Edgar makes him a not wholly attractive character, this is perhaps its source. All through the play he shows an instinctive skill in the arts of psychic self-preservation, an adeptness not much more engaging when practised on Gloucester's behalf than on his own. But it is important also to notice that self-preservation means more than just saving his life by assuming a disguise. If it were only that, then any effective disguise would do. The curious, striking jump of 'and am bethought' might suggest a deeper instinct at work, and it emerges clearly in the second half of the speech. To get to the bottom, where one has absolutely nothing to lose, is to be consciously secure, invulnerable in one's visibly total vulnerability: 'The country gives me proof and precedent / Of Bedlam beggars, who . . . / Enforce their charity'. Presented nakedness will 'outface' the worst nature can do, partly by challenging its will to 'persecute' to complete destruction, and partly by anticipating its will to persecute at all. In one sense, therefore, Edgar is not assuming a disguise but stripping himself of the qualities of human civility – including a quality central to his highly articulate, rather 'philosophical' nature, the power to comprehend and to direct experience by means of suitably complex and reflective language. In the hovel, Lear keeps on calling him a 'philosopher', and so indeed he is; as poor Tom, however, he can express his sense of the world only in the most basic minimum terms. And very revealing terms they are, for their very simplicity expresses what impels human nature to seek security in this way.

By and large, Lear's world in these scenes is exactly as dynamic and strife-torn as he is himself. It is magnificent in its total activeness. Even the sheer physicality of things – of the steeples, the 'thick rotundity o' th' world', nature's 'moulds' and 'germens' – is realized by being seen (very actively seen) as itself a kind of resistant action. In short, it is a world answering to both the energy of, and the facts opposing, Lear's will. His mind can seize the energies nature generates by conflict, and can identify itself with them, if only he can feel they have some point – a direction, an intent – whether it is to punish the wrong-doing of others or to test his own power of endurance. He is struggling to find a purchase in reality both for his will and for a 'justice' that would discharge it; and the struggle mounts through these scenes until it discloses the real end it has been bound to. The impulse to act energetically in and on the world, which in Lear is the need both to realize an essential capacity of the self and to make 'justice' an objective reality, can *of itself* only issue in something like the mock-trial: paranoia, fantasies of persecution, lies, murderous rage, and a coldly vicious brutality:

> Arraign her first; 'tis Goneril . . . she kick'd the poor King her father . . .
> Arms, arms, sword, fire! Corruption in the place! . . .
> The little dogs and all . . . see, they bark at me . . .
> Then let them anatomize Regan, see what breeds about her heart . . . (III, vi, 46ff)

And as I have suggested, the blinding of Gloucester promptly deals with any thought we might have that this is only a fantasy revealing a merely subjective truth about Lear. That scene exhibits the objective reality of 'the thick rotundity o' th' world' being struck flat, and none the less so because the energy of the striking also makes objectively real the 'thick rotundity' it meets – physically, of Gloucester's eyes, and morally, of his capacity to stand at last in a due resolution and endure the necessary cost.

But if one 'true need' of humanity – for action and 'justice' – is represented in Lear, the storm-scenes place others beside it: the loyalty and folk-sense represented in the Fool, the wavering but finally undeniable spark of human kindness in Gloucester, and the particular kind of 'patience' represented in Edgar as Tom:

poor Tom . . . whom the foul fiend hath led through fire and through flame, through ford and whirlpool, o'er bog and quagmire; that hath laid knives under his pillow, and halters in his pew; set ratsbane by his porridge; made him proud of heart, to ride on a bay trotting-horse over four-inch'd bridges, to course his own shadow for a traitor. Bless thy five wits! Tom's a-cold. O! do de, do de, do de. Bless thee from whirlwinds, star-blasting, and taking! Do poor Tom some charity, whom the foul fiend vexes. There could I have him now, and there, and there again, and there. (III, iv, 50ff)

Tom's is a world in which ordinary everyday things are not
forms of energy as they are for Lear. Although they are
simply themselves – material, neutral objects – they can at
the same time be 'charged', as it were, with a terrifying
menace: a menace all the more mysterious and yet all the
more real because they are so commonplace. It is a world
where magic and witchcraft would flourish, where one's
own 'shadow' could be a traitor. That particular image has
a powerful relevance to the whole play, of course, but for
Edgar/Tom the shadow's threat comes from no merely
human agency. If it did, it might be countered by human
action. Rather, human beings are either vessels or victims
of 'the foul fiend', of a principle of sheer evil so powerful
that only one thing is left for men to do: 'take heed of the
foul fiend', 'defy the foul fiend', 'prevent the foul fiend', and
'bless thee from star-blasting and taking'. The world is
metaphysically determined; humanity can only suffer its
onslaught from without or within ('poor Tom . . . that
in the fury of his heart, when the foul fiend rages, eats cow-
dung for sallets'), trying to hold to the one simple moral
code it knows in a cold world:

Take heed o' th' foul fiend. Obey thy parents; keep thy word's
justice; swear not; commit not with man's sworn spouse; set not
thy sweet heart on proud array— (III, iv, 80ff)

. . . defy the foul fiend. Still through the hawthorn blows the cold
wind— (*ibid.*, 99–100)

Beyond that, men can only pray for deliverance. As seen by
Tom, values are essentially given and essentially dualistic.
More importantly, the world is essentially unalterable by
human action, as though all activity in it were initiated by
some evil spirit whose visitations we can in the end only
wait to pass by, to be replaced perhaps by a good one.

'Pray, innocent, and defy the foul fiend.' There is thus the directest line between Tom's wholly negative morality ('obey . . . keep . . . swear not . . . commit not . . . set not') and Edgar's view that 'ripeness is all'. Men must endure; even though the foul fiend rages within their hearts, they are essentially acted *upon*.

Clearly, the world evoked and represented by Tom/ Edgar is so real that the corresponding human 'need' – a kind of wary goodness, a patient evading of evil – is no less 'true' than the energetic power of Lear's. We often do see life as Tom sees it: dominated by powers of light and darkness that come and go unaccountably. And in Goneril and Regan, to look no further, we do see an evil apparently irreducible and inexplicable. It seems to be simply *there* – and in the face of it we seem able only to ask as helplessly as Lear, 'is there any cause in nature that makes these hard hearts?', without any real expectation of an answer. Indeed, in the last analysis the whole play seems to prompt some such attitude as this. Bradley's view of it, for example, has something of Edgar's spirit in it, and he expresses a common and perfectly natural reaction when he too regards its world as one whose ultimate terms are good and evil – exclusive absolutes that are somehow just mysteriously given, and whose burden therefore has finally to be just patiently accepted. And yet if that is obviously true enough in one way, it is a truth that (as John Danby has observed of the thunder in these scenes)[1] can mean very different things. All depends on the spirit in which it is seen, on what other truths are seen as well, and on the particular emphasis given it by that context. The word 'patience', as we have noticed, can be attached to various attitudes, some more adequate to the full range of human possibilities than others. Perhaps

[1] Danby, *Shakespeare's Doctrine of Nature*, pp. 181ff.

it is worth recalling Johnson's love of justice at this point, for if Bradley has something of Edgar's spirit, Johnson has something of Lear's. We want more – want to *do* more – than just wonder at the mystery of hard hearts, or even just try to evade the foul fiend; and the play prompts that impulse in us even though – or more precisely, because – we recognize any such 'cause in nature' at work in Lear as well as in all three of his daughters.

The need Tom/Edgar represents is not offered to us as more 'true' than Lear's; in fact, some of the sharpest ironies in the play are reserved for Edgar, almost as if Shakespeare felt slightly irritated by such adept, talkative, but fundamentally self-protective moralism. But the storm-scenes merely expose it to the impact of Lear's 'need'. Significantly enough, it is the madness to which Lear's energy finally comes in its search for an answering principle of justice, that causes Edgar, who can see a moral principle in the world all right but no positive principle of human energy, finally to break down:

> My tears begin to take his part so much,
> They mar my counterfeiting.
>
> Tom will throw his head at them. Avaunt, you curs!
>
> . . . Poor Tom, thy horn is dry   (III, vi, 60ff)

When it comes to the pinch, he is not so much unable to find anything to say, as unable to restrain the impulse to act. It is already possible to see why Edgar is the most lethal character in the play. Later on, the man who proclaims one moment that he is

> A most poor man, made tame to Fortune's blows;
> Who, by the art of known and feeling sorrows,
> Am pregnant to good pity—   (IV, vi, 222–4)

finds the next moment that (for the best of reasons) he has to kill Oswald. He is the one who (likewise) kills Edmund, and who (likewise again) kills Gloucester. It is no empty irony that in the storm-scenes he helps to start Lear into madness by suddenly looming in the darkness like an evil spirit. There is a revealing moment in the hovel when Lear asks 'this same learned Theban',

> What is your study?
> EDG. How to prevent the fiend, and to kill vermin.
>
> (III, iv, 161–3)

In Edgar's world as in himself, that disjunction between 'prevent' and 'kill' is no less clearly marked and (because unacknowledged and unreckoned with) no less devastating than those in Lear's.

III

Viewed as a whole, the significance of this third Act lies in the many-sided dramatic image of 'true need' it presents – presents with such marvellous intensity, subtlety of resource, and organic unity – rather than in any spiritual change it traces in Lear. To put the emphasis on Lear's awareness or sufferings, or to want to put it there – as though what chiefly mattered were what the hero comes to realize rather than what the work comes to realize, and us with it – is either to risk sentimentalizing him, since in fact he shows little spiritual progress in Act III, or to conclude from that fact, as Mr Mason does (even though he remarks 'we are made to ponder on *all* that happens in this . . . act, not merely on Lear's soliloquies'), that Shakespeare has confused the action with Lear's moral 'posturings', and the only serious treatment of evil, suffering, and spiritual development now centres on Gloucester.[1] The action

---

[1] Mason, *Shakespeare's Tragedies of Love*, pp. 194ff.

moves less to any discovery made in or through Lear's awareness about the nature of Evil or the nature of Nature, than to what his awareness itself, or rather his uncontrollable fantasies, his confused grapplings with his experience – together with everything else in the Act – exhibit of the impulses and needs at work in him as in others. Nor is he shown to us as a man being purged of illusion and guilt by a sort of metaphysical or spiritual 'storm'. He is a man breaking into pieces in a real storm, which *to him* inevitably seems to manifest a world breaking itself, or him, or both, into pieces.

Far from inviting us to ignore Lear's inner confusions, the action insists on them. If there are signs of a new honesty and insight being born in him, this does not account for the tremendous force of his speeches. The force is that of a shattering inner explosion; and the process uncovers not the truth about Nature, but (more provisionally) the apparently inescapable contradictions in him, the very intensity of which cause the explosion. The full dramatic effect actually depends on our noticing all the weaknesses in Lear: the fact, for instance, that he is riddled with self-pity and self-delusion, and driven by a terrifying destructive violence; that the man who can display himself in such pyrotechnics is not altogether 'a poor, infirm, weak, and despis'd old man'; that, although he suffers and endures no more easily than anyone else might, his cry of pain – 'more sinned against than sinning' – is not the whole truth; that it wouldn't answer even if he could manage to be 'the pattern of all patience' and 'say nothing'; and that if only now does he begin to realize how little 'poor naked wretches' have to protect them against the storms of life – an observation (as other critics have already remarked) not so free from self-pity and self-regard as to be an especially convincing sign of a new and profound compassion at work in him – then he could hardly have been the 'kind old father' whose frank heart gave all, or now be the man to call for punishment on the 'close-pent guilts' of others. His own heart may have been 'frank' at least in spontaneously intending good, which neither Goneril's nor Regan's is; but it was hardly unpent enough, to others or itself, to have given *all*. To cry as he does for the 'all-shaking thunder' to strike flat the world and destroy 'ingrateful man', is for the self to run distractedly from one threat to another, to face a bear in order to avoid the roaring sea, or (more accurately) for his mouth to tear his own hand for lifting food to it (III, iv, 6ff). In short, if he is not learning a redeeming wisdom in these scenes, neither is he merely 'posturing'. He is going mad. Thus when Tom first appears, Lear does not identify himself with the poor naked wretch in an access of new-found understanding; he identifies the wretch with himself: 'Did'st thou give all to thy daughters? / And art thou come to this?' (III, iv, 48–9). When he does identify himself with Tom a little later, it is by then quite clearly an act of madness, the sense of helpless injury driving him to deprive himself of everything rather as Edgar did. But Lear does so out of a significantly divided impulse – partly to 'justify' his obsessive, limitless sense of injury, and partly to satisfy his correspondingly obsessive urge to 'punish home':

> Death, traitor! nothing could have subdu'd nature
> To such a lowness but his unkind daughters . . .
> Judicious punishment! 'twas this flesh begot
> Those pelican daughters. (III, iv, 70ff)

And the same divided impulse also drives him to the famous speech about 'unaccommodated man':

Thou wert better in a grave than to answer with thy uncover'd body this extremity of the skies. Is man no more than this? Consider him well. Thou ow'st the worm no silk, the beast no hide, the sheep no wool, the cat no perfume. Ha! Here's three on's are sophisticated; thou art the thing itself; unaccommodated man is no more but such a poor, bare, forked animal as thou art. Off, off, you lendings! Come; unbutton here. (*ibid.*, 103ff)

IV

This latter speech is so often taken as a profound and central truth about man, which Shakespeare has given his hero to 'see' (on our behalf, as it were), and Lear's understanding of it so often taken as an important step in his spiritual development, that it is worth considering it in some detail.

In the first place, it is hard to see, even in the light of Lear's earlier speech about 'true need' at the end of Act II (to which this obviously relates), that what Lear himself means here is especially profound. This view of things does represent a change in him, as I think we feel, though a masked and highly qualified one; but such insight as the speech discovers to us is of a kind Lear himself is visibly incapable of – that, in fact, being a vital part of it. For the insight is not spoken to us by Lear so much as embodied to us in his actual presence, and it can be grasped only in those terms – this man in this situation and uttering these particular words, struggling desperately, in his own particular way, to divide the indivisible both in himself and in his world. The total dramatic reality of his saying what he does exhibits yet another side of the same paradox as everything else in these scenes: that no one human necessity is paramount, nor can it be separated from the rest without losing its validity, its 'truth' as a need of the self.

All through these scenes, we notice, Lear can realize the powers of nature as hostile to human activities only by paradoxically endowing them with human-like intent ('thought-executing fires', 'vaunt-couriers', 'pitiless storm', and so on). He can think of humanity only by endowing it with the solidity and energy of nature ('caitiff, to pieces shake', 'close pent-up guilts, / Rive your concealing continents'). He can see nature in terms of powerfully destructive gods only by seeing it as also self-destructive ('crack Nature's moulds'), and yet only see this in turn by seeing its energies as also creative – not merely in the 'germens' they might spill, but (as 'dreadful summoners') in shaping moral justice in the very substances (oaks or human minds) that embody their power. Nor can he even conceive these powers as 'just' – and so to be endorsed, identified with, released in himself – without also conceiving them as so terrible and so alien to humanity that man can only tremble at them, protect himself by his arts against them, and in the extremity try to 'bide' their onslaught. The sheer energy of Lear's speeches – together with all the inter-related characters, attitudes, actions, images, surrounding them – exhibits how little anyone, being at once part of 'objective' reality and 'subjectively' apart from it, can define his self either in speech or action, without the terms, the felt substance, of nature. He must see it as the external reality creating and shaping that self, and as that to which he must therefore accommodate; he must equally see it as what the self must act upon in order to make that accommodation. Moreover, just as the inner reality of any of these 'true needs' can be apprehended only in terms of all the rest, so the outward reality of the world itself can only be apprehended in terms of to-and-fro conflicting elements, and the reality of those again only in terms of each other.

Thus in the speech about 'unaccommodated man', it is we who notice the ambiguities in 'answer' and 'extremity', for instance, as Lear cannot. Likewise it is we who see the self-defeating paradoxes he is struggling with, which extend, beyond the anomalies he does see, to embrace also the reasons and effect of his seeing them in that way. This is not to say that those he does see are irrelevant to the action. On the contrary, they have an obvious bearing on what has happened already and is happening now in the storm. It is one of Lear's own points, for example, that the silk, the hide, the wool, the perfume – the 'clothes', the 'arts of necessity', which distinguish man from the beasts – are actually drawn from the beasts. Man needs them even for his animal existence, and yet also for his dignity as man, since they are 'superfluous' to his mere naked animality; but yet again, it is man's animal-like greed that makes him want more than the dignity of his nature strictly needs. Again, Lear sees well enough – even if only implicitly – that man's very capacity to accommodate himself to the physical world, his rationality, is what enables him to prey on his fellow creatures in order to protect himself from the physical world: that in fact he needs to exercise his rationality in order to resist the very circumstances tending to frustrate it. One might untangle even more from his words, but none of it would rise higher than the level of familiar, if pointedly relevant, commonplaces, since that is all they can mean to Lear. To him, the main import of his sight of Tom's wretchedness, of his own words, and of his move to take off his own clothes too, is only to declare how pitifully small, but how pitilessly denied, are human needs in a world that at once endorses them as true needs and yet denies them, and by declaring that, to challenge that world with his own superior sense of 'justice'.

In what *we* see, however, the paradoxes in Lear's consciousness are caught up in a larger, more complex, and yet more specific import; indeed, they become the medium in which it assumes dramatic reality. To start with, there is the significant fact that Lear cannot even think of man as an animal except by not allowing himself to think of the very thing that makes him more than an animal – his capacity to think. To put it another way, he can conceive man only as that kind of animal that uses 'clothing' and other 'arts' – whether to protect itself or to disguise its 'truly' animal nature from itself. Implicitly, he has to conceive man as the animal capable of self-deception; but that, of course, also implies the capacity of self-understanding; and as we notice this, his speech begins to reveal its desperate self-negations. What generates all the imagery of 'clothes' and gives it dramatic point is essentially the same paradox embodied in his remark a little earlier, that 'the art of our necessities is strange, / And can make vile things precious' (III, ii, 70–1). The very 'art' to use them, and the 'art' to judge them vile or precious (or, for that matter, to judge any set of circumstances to be an 'extremity') – that is to say, the capacity to value and to seek meaning – are both equally 'necessities' of human nature, and are so just because of the 'necessities' laid upon it from outside by the physical world it inhabits and to which it needs must 'answer'.

In this speech, Lear's need to 'answer' those externally imposed necessities is made visible precisely by the 'arts' to which it drives him – the 'philosophical' generalities, the need to *declare* his 'true' reality. Equally, the inner needs implicit in his answer – to assert and *justify* his 'true' reality, and yet at the same time to mask the consciousness of his ultimate helplessness by making such grandiose gestures and assertions – are made visible in the way he conceives the necessities apparently laid upon him from outside. The touch of frenzy in his words only sharpens our sense of the various human needs struggling to realize them-selves within him. The need to find meaning in life both manifests and contradicts itself in his effort to prove that man is *merely* 'a poor, bare, forked animal'. The need to will and to act in accordance with values manifest in the objec-tive world both manifests and contradicts itself in his chal-lenging the world to show that it cannot be challenged because it is controlled by a 'will' all-powerful and yet utterly indifferent to all values. And the need to protect his deepest vulnerability – which lies not in the meagre frailty of his body, but in his capacity to feel, to will, to want meaning and justice – again both manifests and contradicts itself in his declaring, in the midst of his pain, that he really needs nothing to protect him from the world.

That Lear is largely moved by self-pity and self-will is an essential part of his dramatic reality; but that should not lead us to wash our moral hands of him. His pain and his attempt to meet it are none the less real, and none the less significantly human, for that. What frustrates his attempt to meet his pain is the inability to acknowledge its real source or even its actual presence. As we can see, it is not his body he needs to bare to the elements, but his self to its own acceptance. The real helplessness of his 'heart' is what he is helpless to acknowledge. To us, his clothing is only a metaphor for the mask by which he conceals and protects himself from any deeper self-awareness – the self-defensive idea of himself as a good man unjustly treated. Indeed, clothing being no mere metaphor to him, all his talk about it is an example of the very thing it represents to us: a guise to conceal and flatter reality. Thus his eagerness to strip himself, to bare the 'reality', just because it is a substitute kind of exposure, reveals how little he can endure to face the true reality. And yet there is still his desperate impulse to expose his reality, even though it is only a substitute kind of exposure: an impulse that reveals equally how little he can endure not to know that reality.

In the immediate dramatic context – where we take these points almost instinctively or unawares as we respond – his words and actions reveal themselves as the only 'clothing' in which he can make the truth visible to himself so as to grasp any of it at all, and at the same time the only way he can muffle it so as to bear any of it at all. If (like any human 'art' or 'fiction') they distort and thus conceal the naked truth, they also make it manifest; and by doing so in one way to him, they do so in another way to us. The basic truth we see here – both in what he can realize of himself and in what he cannot – is not so much the mere fact of his various, conflicting 'needs', as the basic capacity without which they would not be 'true' needs at all (nor, in fact, without which could we see them as such): the distinctive human capacity to feel. Were it not for that in him, reality would need no art or clothing, since he would be insensible of, and thus totally invulnerable to, any insult, injustice, or rejection. These would appear no 'extremity' requiring an 'answer', nor would the one thing he cannot bear to acknowledge – the feeling of his own human vulnerability to these things. The more intensely he feels, in fact, the more he is involved in self-contradiction to deny the pressure – the very capacity to *be* himself both pushing him towards feeling, and pulling him away from it, until his very elements fly apart.

Indeed, the whole world presented throughout this Act is one of which every element, including the human figures in it, necessarily depends on the rest for its very identity, and yet the reality of which seems to flash out most vividly in the differences and conflicts between them, in a strife so intense that it turns into 'images of revolt and flying off'. What is true of the elements of nature and its conflicting aspects is equally true of the differing elements within the individual, and of the elements in mankind that are distributed here among the individual characters, whose particular flaws and limitations are as important a part of their dramatic meaning as of their dramatic reality. The element in man that (most clearly in Lear) 'needs' an answering moral order, 'justice', seems to become most intensely real and active just when the will, pressed by its own helplessness, drives itself against the world in a blaze of mad disorder. The element which (in Tom) needs to 'outface' evil by avoiding all but evasive action, seems most real and active just when it collapses into the impulse to protect another. And the element which (in the Fool) needs only to adjust to a commonsense view of life, seems most real and active just when it collapses into a loyalty and a buoyancy of spirit that go beyond all commonsense. In Act III, each of these individuals – and Kent and Gloucester as well – is driven to encounter the world, and therefore his self, to its very limit. And what happens in the blinding-scene at the end of the Act is only the most obvious, the climactic example of what is exhibited all through it. To put it in general terms is to make it sound impossibly abstract, especially when the whole point is that it is to be seen only in particulars; what is more, it is inevitably to separate insights whose very force depends upon their being embodied in dramatic, and therefore organic, connection. But it is as if the human, as distinct from the god-like or the bestial, were discovered to consist – or rather, to be visible – only in a number (though of course not an exhaustive number) of particular yet incompatible 'needs', and because of that, to be realizable only in *individuals* – in particular but necessarily limited configurations of 'need'. Each configuration defines the very identity of the individual self, though the individual can identify himself consciously only in the 'needs' he can see and acknowledge; and he tries to protect that identity, by inner precautions and stratagems, from 'needs' whose presence he feels obscurely threatening from beyond its limits. But in the end the humanity of each self is revealed, not only in the strength it musters in this way to master life or at least cope with it, but in its most deeply hidden and subtly defended capacity to answer to it – the necessary ability, that is, to *break*.

5

Answering and questioning

Where the main effect of Act III is to discover some of man's
basic necessities, Act IV (I have suggested) is predomi-
nantly concerned with how he might think about and act
upon them; it forms an intensely dramatic tissue of reflection, in which the scenes of Lear's madness (vi) and of his
reconciliation with Cordelia (vii) both give and take particular force. Its second scene, for instance, in which Albany
is jolted into action, is obviously related to the first, in
which Edgar is given an appalling jolt just when *his* rather
'cowish spirit' is philosophically congratulating itself on
being now so low and dejected that he has nothing to
fear:

> Welcome, then,
> Thou unsubstantial air that I embrace:
> The wretch that thou hast blown unto the worst
> Owes nothing to thy blasts.   (IV, i, 6–9)

His own word 'unsubstantial' suggests the obvious comment
on invulnerability such as this – a comment immediately
made explicit, of course, by the entry of Gloucester, blinded
and helpless, with all the anguish he feels and the anguish
he prompts Edgar (and us) to feel. But in shattering Edgar's
feeling of security, Gloucester's entry also underlines again
how much the substance of life actually consists in just such

possibilities of horror and pain as Edgar is seeking to avoid.
Edgar's response is equally revealing:

> O Gods! Who is 't can say 'I am at the worst'?
> I am worse than e'er I was.   (*ibid.*, 25–6)

It is wholly characteristic of Edgar that he should reflect
on man in this way. The human capacity to know and define
one's experience in words does enable, as it also needs, a
degree of reflective detachment, and yet somehow life
keeps breaking in. It is equally characteristic of him, however, not to acknowledge how much reflection, or even
consciousness itself, may protect the self against being
wholly and intensely alive. The 'philosophic' mind can
'tame' one's experience of its most painful, savage, extreme,
contradictory aspects – its power to destroy the recognizable self – by filtering out these aspects before they can *be*
experienced. Albany, we recall, looked to the heavens to
'tame these vilde offences'; Gloucester's spirit is cowed or
tamed to philosophic resignation before the 'opposeless
wills' of the gods; as Tom, Edgar seems to Gloucester one
who is 'humbled to all strokes' (IV, i, 65), and declares
himself later to be 'tame to Fortune's blows' (IV, vi, 222):
for all of them the very idea of 'taming' arises from within a
state of conscious 'philosophic' reflection *about* life or about
themselves. Beside the idea of 'taming', and the related impulse towards humility before the chances of life, the
action places not only the impulse in Albany's very flesh to
seek revenge, or Edgar's need to despatch Oswald, or
Gloucester's urge to kill himself, but also the ravings of
Lear, the possibilities embodied in Cordelia, and the
vibrant *stasis* of the reconciliation scene.

The entry of the mad Lear in Act IV, scene vi, comes,
like Gloucester's in scene i, promptly after a piece of

philosophizing by Edgar. The irony is too obvious to miss; yet it does not consist (as is sometimes supposed) in a discrediting of Edgar's philosophy, but rather, as with Lear's speeches in the storm-scenes for example, in the way his philosophy both manifests and contradicts the realities to which it tries to answer. At first the effect does seem merely negative. The reality of Lear's madness, although it does not wholly reduce Edgar to silence (nothing does quite), does reduce him to the language of sheer pain: 'O thou side-piercing sight!', '. . . it is, /And my heart breaks at it' (IV, vi, 85, 142-3). Edgar's previous interchange with Gloucester had put a view so humane, so answerable to the inter-dependence of man and the world he inhabits as we have actually seen it in Gloucester's case, that it might then have seemed the only convincing possibility:

> It was some fiend; therefore, thou happy father,
> Think that the clearest Gods, who make them honours
> Of men's impossibilities, have preserved thee.
> GLOU. I do remember now; henceforth I'll bear
> Affliction till it do cry out itself
> 'Enough, enough', and die . . .
> EDG. Bear free and patient thoughts. But who comes here?
>
> (IV, vi, 72ff)

Clearly, Edgar's attitude here represents an advance on trying merely to forestall life. All the same, Lear's very first words – 'No, they cannot touch me for coining; I am the king himself' – fall with an equally clear and devastating impact on the weakness inherent in 'think' and 'bear . . . thoughts'. For one thing, Lear's madness is too shockingly real to be annihilated to 'thoughts', however free and patient; nor, for that matter, does it offer very convincing evidence of 'the clearest Gods'. Again, he *is* the king, and (as his assertion of it reminds us) how can a king – bound as he is to rule, to act, to judge, to punish, and to stamp his own image on coin so as to attest its value for everyone – bear only free and *patient* thoughts? Moreover, the metaphorical force of 'coining' bears directly on the suggestion in Edgar's words that a man can choose what kind of thoughts to bear, can stamp whatever image he likes upon the world. For what man is 'king' of reality, to make the thunder cease at his bidding? As Lear remarks – and his very madness exhibits the point – 'Nature's above art in that respect'.

For all Lear's detachment from the world he generalizes about, he is mad – mad precisely in being so detached from it that his thoughts are not free, even if they do have a ghastly sort of patience. What he says may have a kind of 'reason in madness', as Edgar puts it; but he is too insanely 'objective', too alienated, to see more than a part of the truth, just as it is less than the whole of himself whose image is stamped upon it. A man's attitude to women generally reflects his attitude to life itself (or maybe it is the other way around), and although Lear has reason enough for his fear and hatred, these feelings clearly represent a self-closing against the very possibility of giving or receiving love. Desperate for invulnerability against everything to which love leaves him open, he has to see the world as utterly incapable of love at all. Seeing it therefore as only a bestial, nihilistic riot of appetite and hypocrisy, he can also insist that, since it cannot be tamed, it must be tolerated. Both the vision and the precept arise from the same cause: even though he feels imprisoned in the world, he feels himself – has to feel himself – ultimately uninvolved in it. In his savage cynicism, he assumes a clear, simple, black-and-white, and quite *absolute* split between a 'lower' (objective) reality and 'higher' (subjectively held) values –

an assumption very common no doubt, and which often seems justified, but which is none the less insane in its ultimate, and destructive, falsity. The difference within Lear himself between what he has to feel and know on the one hand, and what he can allow himself to feel and know on the other – the pressure of both being inescapable, 'needs' he cannot reconcile and which he therefore needs to split apart in himself in order to survive at all – and the split he 'finds' in the 'objective' world, answer to each other:

> Ay, every inch a king:
> When I do stare, see how the subject quakes.
> I pardon that man's life. What was thy cause?
> Adultery?
> Thou shalt not die: die for adultery! No:
> The wren goes to 't, and the small gilded fly
> Does lecher in my sight.
> Let copulation thrive . . .
> Down from the waist they are Centaurs,
> Though women all above:
> But to the girdle do the Gods inherit,
> Beneath is all the fiend's: there's hell, there's darkness,
> There is the sulphurous pit – burning, scalding,
> Stench, consumption; fie, fie, fie! pah, pah!
> Give me an ounce of civet, good apothecary,
> To sweeten my imagination . . . (IV, vi, 110ff)

If this 'imagination' of the world is too harshly particular to be wholly false, it is too harshly dualistic to be wholly persuasive either – whether about Gloucester or women or sexual love. The world Lear sees here is one we may recognize – one without shame, where monsters of the deep would devour each other with relish, and which holds no possibility of being tamed except by a power outside it. Nor is it hard to see the twisted logic behind his moral conclusions: 'let copulation thrive', 'none does offend', 'thou

137

must be patient'. Because it is also the 'fiend's' world, it can evince no 'clearest Gods' nor any possibility of bearing '*free and patient thoughts*'; indeed, being so much more intense, detailed, and specific than Tom's or Albany's vision, it is also more convincing than theirs. And yet it is finally unconvincing for just the same reason as theirs: it omits the crucial fact of an Albany or an Edgar or a Lear being also within it; it is not conceived in patience. The distortion in Lear's vision is itself the mark of outrage – of a highly *un*tamed, *un*patient revulsion from a world whose falsity and evil he cannot bear except by seeing the world as fit only for total rejection. It is the mark, that is, of the pain, the 'offence', it does give men – the offence they find so unendurable that in their very rejection of it lies the possibility of the world being 'tamed' (if that is the word) from within itself. Seizing on a 'Nature' that apparently defies all the human arts of accommodation, Lear's spirit is driven mad precisely because it cannot morally accommodate itself to it. If only he realized that his own capacity for outrage and suffering (and others' too: Gloucester, who brought him comfort in the storm, is there in front of him) are themselves part of the world – if, in other words, he could *think* about it differently – then he would see it as able to support freer and more patient thoughts. The only trouble is that he cannot think of it that way; and as we remember that the precepts about 'thinking' come from Edgar, the irony doubles on itself. In so far as a man *can* choose to bear free and patient thoughts, it proves his capacity to act – but proves it to an almost trivial end, since the result is so likely to be 'wishful' thinking or a patience that tries to accept more than it really can. In so far as he cannot so choose, however, the only way he can come to think differently is for his whole self to be moved by internal or external powers – the gods, perhaps, or the fiend: a result they usually effect by jolting him painfully from one state into another. But then, we may well ask (and Edgar himself prompts the question as much as anyone: even his exclamation here as he beholds Lear's insanity – 'and my heart breaks at it' – raises it), do men not subtly choose to bear all kinds of thoughts, even free and patient ones, to protect themselves from just such powers and such jolts into chaos? Indeed, do they not *need* to?

Thus the reality we are given in Lear and his world at this point neither confirms nor refutes Edgar's 'philosophy'. Rather, it re-affirms and at the same time qualifies the human truth evident in the particulars of *Edgar's* holding it and at *this* point. Just as Albany was himself one of the only 'visible spirits' the heavens will send, and Edgar's own preservation of Gloucester from suicide was itself the only 'clear' evidence of the 'clearest' Gods, so with Lear's capacity to weep. Exemplifying the capacity in man at once to suffer the world and reject it, to accept it in patient sorrow and yet at the same time to attack it in thought or action so as to fashion order and meaning in it, it itself shows men as 'fools' of reality and at the same time reality as more than a 'stage of fools':

> If thou wilt weep my fortunes, take my eyes;
> I know thee well enough; thy name is Gloucester;
> Thou must be patient; we came crying hither:
> Thou know'st the first time that we smell the air
> We wawl and cry . . .
> When we are born, we cry that we are come
> To this great stage of fools . . .   (IV, vi, 178ff)

There is an almost unbearably painful, and completely sane, feeling of human fellowship in the first and (even more) the second line here, a tone notably different from

that in the rest of the speech, even from the icy calm barely
covering the self-lacerating pain and despair of the following line – though it is not so different, significantly, from
the simplicity of 'Come on, my boy. How dost, my boy?
Art cold?', or from the more securely held note of 'For, as I
am a man, I think this lady / To be my child Cordelia'. To
'think' like that – acknowledging the individual and yet
common human reality of others – is for Lear not so much
to recognize, as more fully to *be* himself, and in a spirit
which is neither 'tame' nor 'untame', since it is both pur-
posefully active and yet vulnerably open in a form of life
that transcends any word like 'tame'.

Obviously, though, Lear cannot sustain the human spirit
of those lines at this point – the question being, indeed,
whether anyone can really ever do so. The need to reject
the world as painfully alien (to 'wawl and cry') and to judge
it ('this great stage of fools') inevitably slides into the need
to do judgment on it, and this in turn into:

> And when I have stol'n upon these son-in-laws,
> Then, kill, kill, kill, kill, kill, kill!   (*ibid.*, 188–9)

a need reinforced a moment or two later, not only by Edgar's
killing of Oswald, necessary as that is to protect the all-too-
vulnerable Gloucester, but by what he discovers from
Goneril's letter. The echo of Lear's earlier speech is tellingly clear:

> To know our enemies' minds, we rip their hearts . . .
>   . . . Here, in the sands,
> Thee I'll rake up, the post unsanctified
> Of murtherous lechers . . .   (*ibid.*, 262, 275–7)

Thus Gloucester's wish for the oblivion of madness at the
very end of the scene,

So should my thoughts be sever'd from my griefs,
And woes by wrong imaginations lose
The knowledge of themselves—   (*ibid.*, 284–6)

becomes, with its repetition of the words 'thoughts' and
'imagination', something like a question, and one relevant
to more than himself. For is this what madness has done for
Lear? – or, to put it perhaps more accurately, what Lear has
had to do for himself by means of madness? – that is, preserved his self, tough though his sides are, from wearing out
to naught in trying to contain the force of *all* its conflicting
'needs'. Has Lear saved himself by madness from trying to
suffer, to act upon, and to acknowledge, the full reality of
his world?

II

Cordelia, in scenes iii and iv, seems to suggest a possible
'better way' than madness or oblivion. She is the daughter
who 'redeems nature from the general curse / Which twain
have brought her to' by realizing its power to restore as
well as to destroy itself. She seems to make its virtues, its
capacity to 'smile', spring with her tears, which answer to
its capacity to storm. The 'art' she represents seems not to
be below nature, but rather, being continuous with nature,
to rise above it. And yet if Lear is in no state to see the significance of Cordelia while he is mad, and was not even while
he was more or less as sane as anybody else, we who see
more need to be careful not to 'think' more into her than is
there. She represents a possibility of reconcilement so
beautiful, so moving, and so desirable that it is easy to let it
swamp our whole consciousness. Real though that possibility is, it is after all only a model, and a miniature one at
that, of a fullness of being which eludes everyone else in the
play, and which, to put it bluntly, eludes her as well. She

reflects it, but she does not encompass it; she embodies its image, its shape, not its full actuality. It is all the more precious for being so rare and so fragile; but as I suggested earlier, it is so fragile because it has to leave so much out:

> Alack! 'tis he: why, he was met even now
> As mad as the vex'd sea; singing aloud;
> Crown'd with rank fumiter and furrow-weeds,
> With hardocks, hemlock, nettles, cuckoo-flowers,
> Darnel, and all the idle weeds that grow
> In our sustaining corn. A century send forth;
> Search every acre in the high-grown field,
> And bring him to our eye.
>   What can man's wisdom
> In the restoring of his bereaved sense?
> He that helps him take all my outward worth. (IV, iv, 1–10)

What the imagination (hers and ours) catches in verse like this is 'sweeter' and no less real than what it seizes in Lear's speech on adultery, for example; but it is no *more* real, and its delicacy, firm as it is, largely depends on encompassing so little of the 'vex'd sea' and of the 'rankness' of those weeds. The weeds seen here as merely 'idle' have in Lear a more savage and intransigent reality. Equally, her tears:

> All bless'd secrets,
> All you unpublish'd virtues of the earth,
> Spring with my tears—

encompass very little of the harsh, stubborn reality of, say, Gloucester's eyes. Her view of war – 'love' and 'right' – leaves out the necessary 'bloodiness'. The doctor's simples do not so much neutralize anguish, much less remove its cause, as 'close its eye':

> Seek, seek for him,
> Lest his ungovern'd rage dissolve the life
> That wants the means to lead it.   (*ibid.*, 15ff)

As we have seen in Act III, sleep, the surrender to oblivion, is needed to preserve a sane consciousness; and yet, for all that it is called 'governing', the 'art' Cordelia represents is one that enables life only by diminishing certain of its possibilities. In truth, it is a kind of 'taming'. No doubt it must be so; nevertheless, it is significant and worth insisting on that even in the reconciliation scene she has to see Lear as merely a victim, and he see in her, even now, only the possibility of '*forgetting* and forgiving'.

These limitations hardly obtrude in the reconciliation scene itself. There, the emphasis is all on the new-born stability of Lear's self facing Cordelia's, each of them now able to acknowledge his own 'need' (or 'bond') of love – which is also to acknowledge his dependence on, his part in, and his vulnerability to, the 'objective' world in which the other exists. The very brevity of Cordelia's speeches to her father is a crucial part of their meaning – that words alone cannot express what she now acknowledges both him and herself to be.

> Sir, do you know me? . . .
>
>   O! look upon me, Sir,
> And hold your hand in benediction o'er me.
> No, Sir, you must not kneel . . .
>
> And so I am, I am . . .
>
> No cause, no cause.   (IV, vii, 48ff)

Each of Cordelia's speeches seems so full of meaning because it is so full of her. Each represents an integral, responsive, completely heart-felt action of the self. Moreover, each powerfully affirms the reality of the person to whom it is addressed. Lear is seen as a simple but profoundly meaningful fact, physical and moral – one that can be acknowledged and answered to only with a 'heart' helplessly vulnerable to his vulnerability, and shamed by the bewildered humility to which shame and helplessness have brought him. To speak this kind of truth does not require many words; in fact the 'heart' would only be betrayed by trying to find them, and the physical reality it confronts only blurred if it succeeded. Beside Cordelia's longer speech at the beginning about 'returning those duties back as are right fit', for example, everything she says here declares a far deeper sense of duty and affirms the 'bonds' of nature far more truly; and it does so because her consciousness is not now trying to fit a supposedly quite private inner self to a supposedly quite objective external reality. Here, all self-consciousness loses itself in her awareness of Lear, just as all self-assertion is transformed into the acts in which she affirms and answers to his reality.

We may call [her condition] love so long as we remember that it is not simply an emotion, and that, although deeply personal, it has also the impersonality that comes from a self-forgetful concentration – momentary or enduring – upon the true being of 'the other' . . . not a negation of personal consciousness but its heightening and fulfilment.

L. C. Knights puts it well.[1] And clearly the only manner in which a 'heart' open at its profoundest level could speak is a stark, direct simplicity like hers here – though there is, we may notice, the other side to it as well, for to express itself fully the 'heart' also needs to act.

Similarly, Lear has little room now for any protective sense of self to corrode his awareness of reality. On the contrary, his awareness of both is at first more lacerating than he can bear:

[1] Knights, *Some Shakespearean Themes*, p. 118.

> You do me wrong to take me out o' th' grave;
> Thou art a soul in bliss; but I am bound
> Upon a wheel of fire, that mine own tears
> Do scald like molten lead.　　　　　　　*(ibid.,* 45–8)

It is from this desperately alienated condition that he is now released, and brought (for the first time) back to a selfhood that might see the world, 'this place', not as hell after all, nor the abode of other souls in bliss, but his 'own kingdom' of men and women. As he awakens, his 'heart' too can use only a direct, naked simplicity of utterance. His speeches move with a wondering, humbled tentativeness, as if reaching out to touch the few bare facts which are all he now possesses of himself and of the world he inhabits:

> I know not what to say.
> I will not swear these are my hands: let's see;
> I feel this pin prick. Would I were assur'd
> Of my condition!　　　　　　　*(ibid.,* 54–7)

Hence the irresistible authority of phrases like 'Pray, do not mock me' or 'Do not laugh at me' or 'Yet I am doubtful' or 'as I am a man': to understand these at all is to answer to them with assent. Even though his speeches seem more than ever to centre on himself, on 'I' and 'me', each 'I' really issues from a question, so that it affirms rather than asserts. It represents not a fragment, nor an evasion, nor a protective role:

> Pray, do not mock me:
> I am a very foolish fond old man,
> Fourscore and upward, not an hour more or less;
> And, to deal plainly,
> I fear I am not in my perfect mind.
> Methinks I should know you and know this man;
> Yet I am doubtful: for I am mainly ignorant
> What place this is, and all the skill I have
> Remembers not these garments; nor I know not

> Where I did lodge last night. Do not laugh at me;
> For, as I am a man, I think this lady
> To be my child Cordelia. (*ibid.*, 59–70)

In Act I, we remember, the speech in which Lear disclaimed Cordelia had moved from the supposedly objective powers of nature ('the sacred radiance of the sun', 'the operation of the orbs') and a correspondingly fragmented sense of himself ('I disclaim all my paternal care', 'a stranger to my heart and me'), to impel the will onward until it discharged itself in the final sundering act of denial: 'thou my *sometime* daughter'. It was a portent of all those later speeches of his that swelled up and exploded with the energy of fission. Here, for the first time, it is the energy of fusion. From the bewildered, fragmented awareness of a world that seems correspondingly fragmented, the speech gradually begins to take a direction in its wandering until it eventually finds its coherence – its heart, as it were – in the final, cohesive acknowledgment. But it is only Lear's ability to acknowledge that 'wheel of fire' as a hell to which he had bound himself within himself, that enables him to be free enough to kneel to another, to beg forgiveness, and to speak with such simple directness out of himself. The self that actually speaks here – able fully to acknowledge all its weakness in age, in folly and ignorance, in its helpless dependence on others even to clothe and lodge it – now possesses the strength to 'deal plainly' with the world. It is able to say 'as I am a man' with humility and doubt, and therefore with justice.

As a whole, therefore, the scene represents a reality quite as irreducible and just as answerable to our sense of life as that represented by the scene of Gloucester's blinding at the end of the previous Act. Each scene realizes an extreme possibility. Humanity, as we saw there, is capable of that, and yet, as we see here, it is also capable of this. It is not after all wholly beyond human reach to speak – even more, to feel and to act – without falsity either to oneself or to others. It is possible to bear at least some of the painful freedom of the 'heart'; and in that condition people can also bear not only to forgive and give love to another, but even to forgive themselves sufficiently to accept it, as they must, from another. One thing that makes all this so deeply moving here is just this sense of emotional release. We have felt what we see here as a possibility from the very beginning of the play, but we have had to see it denied and almost obliterated for so long. Thus when it does come, although it comes unpredictably and at enormous cost, it not only radiates its significance back through all the earlier action; it also becomes a fact that cannot be denied even through everything that follows. Whatever else is possible in human experience, this is, and nothing can annul that fact.

It is no wonder, then, that for many people the whole action of the play should seem to be the progressive revelation of such love and forgiveness as, despite everything, the most fundamental reality of all – just as for others the most fundamental reality of all should seem to be the nihilistic horror of the blinding scene (as of the final deaths). And certainly, if the reality of that horror precludes a wholly 'affirmative' view of the play, the reality of this scene precludes a wholly nihilistic one. Yet in truth the two scenes embody something like the positive and negative poles of the one moral force. They are opposed, but they are also interdependent. The more closely we consider each one the more we are forced to recognize the co-existence of the other reality. Each requires the other, partly as a necessary qualification, but even more to provide the only terms in which it can be defined. The horror of the blinding scene, for example, is not only qualified by the human-kindness of the servants; its horror *is* horror only in relation to the human potentialities realized in such actions as the servants'. So with the love and forgiveness, the pity and self-abnegation of the reconciliation scene. The other side of Cordelia's pity for her father – her angry hostility to her sisters – is more than a qualifying, humanizing touch to her character. Just because it is necessary to make her seem human, it becomes morally significant, for (as we see) human beings can be too callous to feel enmity towards badness as well as too callous to feel pity towards weakness. Cordelia's pity for Lear is morally significant, that is, precisely because his condition justly 'challenged' it, while her sisters' behaviour, like the winds and thunder, justly challenges opposition, enmity. Indeed, Cordelia cannot even express her pity without the terms of warfare: 'challenge', 'oppos'd', 'warring', 'dread-bolted', 'terrible and nimble stroke', '*perdu*', 'helm', 'enemy'. Similarly the 'restoration' and 'repair' she effects are not only qualified by the Doctor's observation:

> Be comforted, good Madam; the great rage,
> You see, is kill'd in him: and yet it is danger
> To make him even o'er the time he has lost; (*ibid.*, 78–80)

the meaning of such 'restoration' and 'repair' can be defined only in relation to 'killing' great rage and to some part of life being really 'lost'. Indeed, the same applies to the whole scene. The power of love and forgiveness in Lear's 'own kingdom':

> You must bear with me.
> Pray you now, forget and forgive: I am old and foolish—
> > (*ibid.*, 83–4)

is significant only in relation to the still felt reality and the still unresolved opposition of other powers:

'Tis time to look about; the powers of the kingdom approach
apace.

The arbitrement is like to be bloody.   (*ibid.*, 93–4)

Because of this it is hard to avoid either exaggerating or
underestimating the significance of the reconciliation scene.
As we see more clearly later in the play, the ability to kneel,
to beg forgiveness, and to speak from the 'heart', does seem
to open quite new possibilities of experience: the possibility
within of a true self-possession, a detachment, an impersonality, which might even enable action by freeing one from
the need to cover and protect the naked self; and the possibility without of a world not of the wren and the small
gilded fly, but perhaps of people who sing like birds, or
kneel and pray, or laugh in happiness, even while taking
upon *themselves* the mystery of things. Nevertheless, in the
reconciliation scene itself this is only a possibility evoked
by what we see, not realized in it. Nor is it even seen by
Lear or Cordelia, much less embodied in either. That does
not make the possibility any the less valuable or any the
less crucial an element in the play; but it does mean that we
have to be wary of giving more dramatic weight to
Cordelia and to Lear's reconciliation with her than these
can truly support. Like father and daughter we are made
profoundly responsive to the 'true need' and to the reality
they now do acknowledge; on the other hand, we are none
the less aware of those they do not – of the energies un-
leashed in the storm-scenes, for example, or of justice and
'arbitrement' – realities that love and a self-accepted nakedness of self have also to encompass, if they can, within their
world of freedom and wonder. Manifestly, those other needs
and realities are not encompassed here. What is manifest is
rather the need and the difficulty of their being so. All that
is so delicately disclosed and surely held in this scene still

leaves much else open; it amounts to no certain resolution. Indeed, since the fact we do see here is so obviously vital to the full being of each person, but so obviously difficult to achieve and to maintain in relation to other true needs and realities, the scene brings us not (as is often supposed) to any basic answer – to a value or a reality more fundamental than any other and therefore capable of withstanding any challenge – but rather to a basic question, a *risk* more fundamental than any other. The scene raises the stakes beyond anything yet; what can be forfeited, we now see, is no less than everything. Certainly, one question in our minds has been, 'is such a possibility as this real? Can people acknowledge such a need?', and that is answered. But only to open another: how far can people bear to acknowledge it? Or to put the question another way, not 'Can this stand against other needs, other possibilities of life?' but 'Can this be fused with them in some mode of being that includes and does justice to them all?' The acknowledgment of this one, we have come to realize, is in a quite literal sense a matter of life and death for the self; but as we have also come to realize, so are others. The very vulnerability to which we respond here, and the fullness and willingness with which we do so, are surely also the grounds on which we begin to fear for it – begin, that is, to feel the pressure, however formless, of a doubt, a question, how far any person can answer to *everything* he needs to acknowledge as real, within and without, in order to be both fully human and fully himself.

III

That there are limits to what Lear and Cordelia can themselves encompass becomes obvious once again after they are captured – in a scene (v, iii) which, significantly again, follows straight on Edgar's philosophizing about ripeness being all. Here, father and daughter seem almost to have exchanged values. She is prepared (in a not very happy phrase) to 'outfrown false Fortune's frown'; patience is oddly transformed by that 'outfrown', and is certainly governed by no spirit of 'forget and forgive' towards her enemies. As always, her tone towards her sisters is one of steely contempt:

> Shall we not see these daughters and these sisters? (v, iii, 7)

Lear, on the other hand, sweeps aside the impulse behind this; and however constrained, it is (and always was) the impulse to do justice. He is now prepared to deny it, to remain aloof from the world, though in a more 'patient' spirit than his earlier insane alienation from it, in order to satisfy the one need he has never been able to acknowledge:

> No, no, no, no! Come, let's away to prison;
> We two alone will sing like birds i' th' cage:
> When thou dost ask me blessing, I'll kneel down,
> And ask of thee forgiveness: so we'll live,
> And pray, and sing . . .

The difference in spirit from the earlier speech on adultery, for example, lies exactly in his assumption now that he and the world are, at least in some degree, part of each other:

> . . . and tell old tales, and laugh
> At gilded butterflies, and hear poor rogues
> Talk of court news; and we'll talk with them too,
> Who loses and who wins; who's in, who's out;
> And take upon's the mystery of things,
> As if we were Gods' spies: and we'll wear out,
> In a wall'd prison, packs and sects of great ones
> That ebb and flow by th' moon. (v, iii, 8–19)

And yet he seems almost eager for that 'wall'd prison', almost as if it were a country retreat. The attraction of

praying and singing and laughing, we notice, depends on
being 'we two *alone*' and 'i' th' *cage*'; his detachment from
the world is an almost gloating feeling of superiority to it.
Beyond the impulse to fulfil his need of love (active and
passive) is also a will to indulge it. The touch of sentimental
unreality about life in 'cages' is the other side of the warm
release of self-approval, and of the accompanying violence,
that immediately follow:

> Upon such sacrifices, my Cordelia,
> The Gods themselves throw incense . . .
> The good years shall devour them, flesh and fell,
> Ere they shall make us weep: we'll see 'em starv'd first.
>
> (*ibid.*, 20ff)

His will now embraces Cordelia; but not only is it still
aggressive, it is still engaged in protecting a particular consciousness of self, even though a self now turned towards a
different kind of need. For the very assumption of spiritual
and physical *in*vulnerability betrays that self as still incomplete: the 'reality' it seizes is significantly incomplete in its
apparently limited power to harm. To suppose that consciousness can use any walls as a bastion to prevent the
world from touching the self, while the self plays on life
from within them as it pleases, is to fall into the kind of
mistake that Marvell explores in *Appleton House*, for example:
any such bastion is necessarily a conscious retreat from
consciousness and is therefore self-frustrating. No walls can
divide up human life so that its happier aspects can be kept
safe on the inside and the unpleasant ones kept outside.
As we soon see, even though the 'they' Lear refers to *are*
devoured by the time they serve, he can be made to weep
none the less.

Cordelia's death repeats for the last time a pattern that
has recurred again and again through the play. It is not a

pattern of random disruption, however; it has had a logic to which we have always had to assent. An aspect of reality answering to one impulse or need, but denied out of another, returns with irresistible power, destroying what the self had conscoiusly made of its world and at the same time restoring, by violently realizing, the possibilities denied in both self and world. Now, the powers that wreaked 'justice' so satisfyingly on Cornwall, Edmund, Goneril, and Regan, irrupt with terrifying suddenness upon the very figure who had represented the possibility that they might be contained within a harmonious fullness of being. The natural violence, which both informs the human impulse to 'justice' and renders it so ambiguous, which was still so alive in Cordelia even though Lear swept it aside, and which was still alive in himself even though he thought only of dismissing the powers of the world, returns with devastating force *upon* her, and, answering to that force, *in* him.

> Howl, howl, howl! O! you are men of stones:
> Had I your tongues and eyes, I'd use them so
> That heaven's vault should crack . . .
>
> A plague upon you, murderers, traitors all . . .
> I kill'd the slave that was a-hanging thee.   (v, iii, 257ff)

The most extreme vulnerability, the cause of tears, and the most extreme need of justice, the cause of anger, destruction and killing, are inseparably wound around each other: visibly in Lear, as they had been from the very start, and in our response in so far as our humanity is alive to his.

To him Cordelia's death is literally shattering. His mind can neither wholly accept nor wholly deny it. He can make nothing of it at all. Even to try to answer to it, the 'marks of sovereignty, knowledge, and reason' are useless; he needs only the most simple, basic human 'knowledge':

> I know when one is dead, and when one lives;
> She's dead as earth . . .

Knowledge of the past, of his faithful Kent, of his other daughters, is irrelevant and unnecessary. And with that, knowledge even of himself crumbles away. For us, his pathetically broken, virtually helpless consciousness testifies to the absolute reality of what it tries to confront. The same is true of his outraged attempt to reject it. And we too look for justice, for if the world makes any sense at all where is the 'justice' of this?

> ALB.   . . . All friends shall taste
> The wages of their virtue, and all foes
> The cup of their deservings. O! see, see!

That was perfectly straightforward; but what could answer to what we now do see, except:

> LEAR And my poor fool is hang'd! No, no, no life!
> Why should a dog, a horse, a rat, have life,
> And thou no breath at all? Thou'lt come no more,
> Never, never, never, never, never!
> Pray you, undo this button: thank you, Sir.
> Do you see this? Look on her, look, her lips,
> Look there, look there!   [*Dies*]

6

Speaking what we can

───

I

In pondering this last scene of the play, nobody can afford to feel very confident of what he sees in it all, much less of putting words to it; but one or two things, even though largely negative ones, are perhaps obvious enough.

In the first place, there is an important distinction between the effect of Cordelia's death on Lear himself and its effect on us. For him it is literally unbearable; for us, although we may well find it almost so, it is not quite unbearable. For Lear Cordelia is 'thou', and her death a fact he has to answer to with his life if he can; for us she is also 'she', and her death a fact to which in the end we have to answer only with our consciousness. The difficulty for him is not the same difficulty as for us, though the two are intimately related and even overlap. We cannot but identify with him, but we are not confronting the mystery of life and death directly as he is. We are, it is true, looking at it through his eyes, but we are also looking at him. He is at least as much part of what we see as is Cordelia's death; and while the action impels us, along with him, to seek some intimation of 'justice' in the world, it also enables us to stand aside sufficiently to see his need of it as itself part of the world of which we seek it. In short, the meaning of the action cannot be simply identified as the meaning, or the lack of it, that Lear sees in his experience.

On the other hand, although we do see Lear's condition objectively, we can hardly describe it as one of self-knowledge achieved through suffering, or a recognition of the moral order he had denied, or a saving reconciliation with it, any more than we could ever truly have described the action in terms of some 'tragic fault' in his character. Such terms may be adequate to other Shakespearean tragedies (though I very much doubt it), but they are certainly not to *King Lear*; nor do we regard Lear at this point, if indeed we ever have, from a position of such superior, clear-eyed moral insight and judgment as is implied by terms like these. On the contrary, the action surely brings us to the same question as life brings him: 'Why should a dog, a horse, a rat have life,/And thou no breath at all?' That he is looking for the gods' meaning, as we might say, and we are also looking for Shakespeare's, is not to presume that Shakespeare has some good answer to Lear's question to give us. Indeed, the very fact that he hasn't is surely part of what he gives us to ponder while we 'obey'.

It ought not to need saying therefore, though evidently it does, that Shakespeare's meaning is not to be found in some special moment of the hero's experience – not even the final one. It would be no answer to the real question, for instance, even if, as Bradley argued, Shakespeare has Lear die believing Cordelia is alive. (Nor of course did Bradley himself suppose it was.) We know Cordelia is not alive; and to take Lear's delusion (though it may be only a hope) as the basis for some final optimism in the play, as some critics do, is really to take the delusion as a kind of personal declaration on Shakespeare's part – an assertion of *his* hope or belief – but one so visibly at odds with the impersonal dramatic facts as to be both gratuitous and sentimental. Nor is it any better to take it simply the other

way round – that is, to see Lear's delusion as the last unpleasant chance, or twist of fate, which breaks him (like
Gloucester) between extremes of grief and joy, and therefore as Shakespeare's assertion of an ultimate pessimism.
Either way we diminish the play by supposing Shakespeare
pushed his thumb into the balance in order to 'communicate' his personal philosophy to the audience. Not merely
is there no objective need to suppose anything of the sort,
but I doubt if we feel any true need to suppose it in our
subjective experience of this scene either. Anyone who can
take Lear's delusion as the expression of Shakespeare's belief is not attending to the immediate drama at all. Like
the play as a whole, the last scene evinces no clear and
certain answers, and it compels our imagination, I would
suppose, largely *because* of that fact.

Finding ourselves returning to this point, therefore, we
may well choose to stop with it. We can at least say of the
play, for example, that Lear's agonized question would not
arise for anyone – certainly would not be felt as agonizing
as it is – if life did evince any clear answer to it. That it comes
so irresistibly not only to his mind but to ours as well, and
yet is left echoing in a void of ambiguous silence, seems the
only truth the play continuously and finally discovers – the
very facts of subjective human experience testifying to
the lack of any 'clearest gods', of any certain objective meaning or Justice that our inner life directly answers to, or even,
with spiritual insight and effort, it might answer to. Seen
from this angle, the action is a series of destructive 'ironies',
abrupt reversals, breaks, sharp disjunctions, each one of
which subtly engages our assent, but which together form
what Frank Kermode would call a gathering 'apocalypse',
a process wherein reality declares itself in the very revenge
it takes upon every belief, upon every expectation or

assertion of meaning or value within which men try to contain it. If that revenge is the only certain 'justice' we see in its world, then our critical emphasis must inevitably fall on such 'ironical' appositions as (to take one crucial instance) that between Albany's declaration of moral and social justice in this final scene and Lear's broken cry; or on the futility of every such moral and social 'fiction' in the play; or on the terrible unfolding 'apocalypse' of the whole; or, if we insist on the world of moral difference revealed between a Goneril and a Cordelia, on the progressive revelation that that world lies within, in the region of human feelings and choices, not without, in the manifest will of any divinities. Some such response to the play is surely understandable, even inescapable; it certainly answers to what is there; and it amounts, putting it bluntly, to denying any final 'affirmation' in the play at all. The great world *does* so wear out to naught. If the dramatic exhibition is not depressing, this is only because of its relentless, unblinking honesty, or because of the feelings of pity and terror it engenders in us for the human grandeur, suffering and defiance represented most notably by Lear, and the goodness, patience and love represented most notably by Cordelia – qualities conspicuously *un*supported by the 'objective' natural world it portrays.

But at this point it is possible to take a further step, and see the play from a different angle altogether. Lear's question has so sharp a point – indeed, it only arises – because it is *this* death and of *this* person. Were the play declaring only the ultimate indifference of Nature, its objective meaninglessness, it would have done so just as clearly had all the main characters killed one another in some conventional hugger-mugger of poison, poniards and poetical ironies. This would not have declared it any more clearly perhaps, but the differences in tone and language between this ending and, say, that of *The Duchess of Malfi* may well remind us that a quite different view of *King Lear* is also understandable, even inescapable, just because it is Cordelia's particular death we find so hard to bear, and because only the starkest simplicity, directness, and integrity could answer to that. We may, like Lear, be so moved by it indeed that we reject it, as Johnson did, as a kind of outrage on Shakespeare's part, a wilful aberration from the meaning his action so far *has* disclosed in life. Or perhaps, as is nowadays more common, we may move further aside from Lear's response in order to observe what is created by means of it, and see his pain and outrage and even his death as all testifying to what causes them: the reality of the values embodied in Cordelia. This perception sometimes moves critics to ejaculations of the utmost sublimity, of course, and no doubt the angelic choir always welcomes a scholarly note or two from the *Shakespeare Quarterly*; but without aspiring to the heights we can recognize that the sense of unbearable loss, which we share with Lear, does arise from the love, integrity and harmony we have glimpsed in Cordelia and which, in some measure at least, have 'redeemed' him too. To consider the play from this angle is thus to see it as an 'affirmation' – or rather, to see it as yielding an affirmation. Despite the all-too-visible evidence of the general curse, the great world can be redeemed from that curse even though never wholly freed of it; and what renders the play anything but depressing is the force this affirmation – that is, both its content *and* its declaration – takes from everything that opposes or seems to oppose it.

It is worth distinguishing this view of the play from that which regards it as merely a philosophical or religious melodrama. This view does at least acknowledge that moral and spiritual values are no simple datum of human experience, visible facts to which the mind has only to adjust itself; and it also credits Shakespeare with enough intelligence to have seen that no simpler faith was available in his own day. Then as now the point Coleridge made about poetry applies to living as well: if a rule could be given from without, the real thing, which continually depends on risking the possibility of defeat, would sink into a virtually mechanical art. Still, values and meaning also depend on facts; some possibilities have more substance than others; and it is a question how much substance is given the 'redemptive' values represented in Cordelia. I have argued that it is not, indeed cannot be, enough to comprehend everything it has to, even in her own self; and turning to the last scene, it is surely relevant that our very sense of loss arises largely from the contrast between the woman who was so formidably alive that she needed to outface 'these daughters and these sisters', and the pathetically immobile body in Lear's arms. Her capacity for 'patience' and the possibilities in nature to which that answers can hardly be said to *contain* all the harsh, disruptive, but immensely powerful vital energies necessary even to her own forceful identity, let alone that of others – Lear's especially. Those energies – informing the very will to assert one's selfhood, to reject the 'given' fact, to demand justice, to act – answer to other, more substantial possibilities in nature.

That, however, offers yet another position from which we may choose to regard the play. Even at the end, for example, we can hardly miss the characteristic, intransigent beat of life in Lear's question, 'Why should a dog, a horse, a rat, have life . . . ?' – the human, as ever, dependent on the vitality it shares with the non-human for the very means to distinguish itself from it. There is a familiar energy even in the last, urgent, necessary out-going of his self: 'Look on her, look . . . ' The insistence on 'justice' – on the world yielding some coherent meaning, some identity – as well as the pressure to act – to make the world answer to one's own needs, one's own self – are still human 'needs' and we still feel them as 'true', here perhaps more than ever. Thus it is no less understandable to regard this manifold vital energy as the predominant reality that the play 'affirms' – or more accurately, that it simultaneously realizes and explores; and to regard the same energy, of which the play itself partakes (since it continually informs its own creative activity), as also the reason why it is never in danger of becoming merely depressing – or, for that matter, in no danger of lapsing into a heart-warming but essentially static Idealism.

Each of these broad types of response can take a number of specific forms, of course, some of which are more adequate than others; but among all the possible (and impossible) views that have been offered of the play, these do at least conform to common sense. That each is so understandable, even so obvious, a way to taking the relevant evidence seems to me a mark in its favour; in fact, I suspect that anyone really attending to the play experiences both the need and the difficulty of somehow holding all three of them at once. And yet I doubt if that is all he experiences. To judge from its relentless hold on our imagination, the ending seems to strike deeper vibrations than any such view accounts for, or even all of them together. If we do feel the need and the difficulty of holding more than any one of them, this is surely not because the play is uncertain or equivocal, nor even because of its ambiguity as a work of art. The reason lies in what it *discloses* rather than what it says; indeed, its ambiguity seems at once a representation and an analogue of some contradiction at the root of human experience itself – one that, growing only deeper the more intensely we try to resolve it, makes it finally impossible to tell whether it lies irreducibly there, as a fact, and has to be accepted (or 'obeyed') as such, or whether it is merely a projection of our inability to master it.

I think we *are* left with a sense that something is 'affirmed' (though that word sounds less than adequate), but if so, this sense is accompanied by another: whatever the 'something' is, it may be impossible to define it. Perhaps this is partly because it is dramatically shown, not merely stated; a more fundamental reason is that it could never properly be stated, since it only exists in the dramatic experience of it; but I believe there is a more fundamental reason still. To define is to specify, to trace limits; and whatever this 'something' is, it seems at once bafflingly specific and yet bafflingly without limits. It is as though our consciousness might bear it as a precipitate from the play, but if so, it would not be the right thing our consciousness possessed; while on the other hand, if we really did possess it, we might then not be able to bear it at all. In one sense, indeed, it seems almost to be the demonstration that, in the intensest experience of life, a definite consciousness of its 'meaning' (even if the 'meaning' seems only the lack of meaning) is impossible. At any rate, the result is that we seem to grope about between some final sense of 'meaninglessness' and 'value' and 'energy' and, beyond that, some intimation so elusive that it disappears as we try to express it, leaving us with perhaps only some forlorn vacuity in our hands – like 'an enhanced and profounder sense of reality' or a 'vibrant sense of life in its fullness', or more words to that general effect.

II

To say anything definite about the final effect of the play and still keep a steady hold on its specific dramatic facts may well be impossible, but as a number of recent critics have argued, those facts do leave us grappling with the sense of some such positive experience or some such insight. It is tempting to call it (as one critic does)[1] 'the ambiguity of human experience' and leave it at that, for up to a point it is that. To risk an obviously imperfect analogy, we might say that the drama shows an ambiguity rather like that of a philosopher's picture-puzzle – the figure of the stairs, for example, to which T. S. Eliot is presumably referring in 'Burnt Norton'. To one view the stairs in the picture are going upwards; to the next they are going downwards; but neither view is a mere illusion, nor is it, while we actually hold it, only a 'fiction'. We know we could see them another way if we chose to, but at this moment we do not, and the stairs really do go upwards. Nor, for that matter, are both views together 'fictions' in any sense that implies we could adopt a view outside these alternatives: the stairs simply do not go sideways, for instance. So perhaps with *King Lear*. Everything absurd or 'grotesque' is really absurd and grotesque, but it is seen in the next glance to be really painful or tragic. Real pain can be seen to be really a blessing, real blessing, pain. Human values are masks or 'clothes' men choose to hide behind; their choice of 'clothes' declares their true values. Evident chance is now evident necessity, or even purpose; then *vice versa*. And so on. The outline of one thing is the boundary of its counterpart. 'Nature' is simple, solid, given; but it declares itself in such utterly conflicting ways that none can be actually taken as final.

[1] Rosenberg, 'King Lear and His Comforters', *Essays in Criticism*, XVI (1966), 146.

And yet if all this is true, it seems only to restate the problem rather than to solve it. We are still left with the peculiar but inescapable *authority* of the last scene to account for, and what its force has to do with the equally inescapable force of Lear's final question.

To get anywhere near these questions, I think we need to remember another point, which tends to be obscured in a term like 'ambiguity' but which the play itself emphatically and continually enforces. To call anything 'ambiguous', even so large a thing as human experience, is implicitly to identify it, to acknowledge it as a single object though with a multiple meaning; but we only need to do this when our experiences are otherwise insupportably discrepant, conflicting, incoherent. It is only because we experience the figure of the stairs, for instance, first as a picture of stairs-going-up, and then as a picture of stairs-going-down, and then reflexively note the discrepancy, and feel the inward need to explain it, that we come to see what we experienced was not two incompatible *pictures* of the same stairs, but really one single, unambiguous *diagram* which illustrates an ambiguity in the conventions of perspective drawing. We are driven to restore our own coherence, our own identity, by finding a coherent identity in the objects of our experience. Nevertheless, the marks on the paper are not more truly the illustration of an ambiguity than they are truly two incompatible pictures: indeed, they would not be the illustration if they were not also two pictures. We can and do experience them as really all three things – but only in turn. To be conscious of them as anything specific at all is actually to *see* them as one of the pictures, or as the other picture, or as the diagram, though as we see any particular one we can be also conscious of the other two as possibilities. Seeking an object of our total consciousness, therefore, we may want to posit a total thing – an entity comprising all three possibilities (and we would probably add the 'marks on the paper' too). Nevertheless, the very conventions that might enable us to experience this putative thing, whatever we call it, as anything specific and determinate, also preclude our realizing it as one total thing. In short, while we can have the experiences or have their relationship – their full meaning, as it were – we cannot have either without some loss of the other; yet since our experience of neither seems complete without the awareness of the other, our consciousness reaches for some third inconceivable thing, which would, without loss, contain both. To many people, of course, this inconceivable something is the Absolute, or the Supreme Fiction, or God.[1]

To say of *King Lear*, then, that it exhibits 'the ambiguity of human experience' is rather like saying that the picture exhibits the ambiguity of the stairs: it is true enough in one way, but inadequate in another. To see the 'human experience' as real, which is how the play makes us see it, we have to see it in its specific, determinate, realized particulars. To see the 'ambiguity' as real, however, we have to shift our mental eye and see every human experience in it as only a possibility. The problem is that we cannot do both simultaneously; and in using the phrase to describe the full reality of the play, we are trying to grasp at some ungraspable total object of our total dramatic consciousness – a consciousness, that is, combining every particular state we

---

[1] Two interesting discussions of related issues are Wittgenstein on the ambiguous duck-rabbit figure, in *Philosophical Investigations*, and E. H. Gombrich on the ambiguity inherent in all three-dimensional representations, in *Art and Illusion*, 2nd ed. (London, 1962), p. 198 and ch. 8. In using the term 'Absolute', incidentally, I have F. H. Bradley especially in mind, many of whose arguments, whatever their validity for the ordinary world, are interestingly relevant to works of art – perhaps especially to works of dramatic art.

share with the characters themselves and our own fuller comprehension of them. True, we do ideally reach towards some such awareness, and we obviously need to try to define what it is the awareness of. But to realize why we feel this need is also to realize its irreconcilability with what prompts it: namely, the need to experience everything in the drama in its *own* specific, yet conflicting, reality. We can talk about 'the ambiguity of human experience' only in abstract terms, as if the whole were present to us at once. This does not make the ambiguity we see any the less real, but it does prevent our doing justice to the reality of *this* experience and *that* experience – to the particularities, that is, and their sequence in time, in virtue of which human experience *is* human experience. In the end, I suspect, about the only adequate thing we could say of the drama as a whole is that it exhibits our own anomalous position here, for as the characters in it stand to 'nature', so do we, but so do we also stand to them. At least this seems to me why (as critics have sometimes remarked) our own capacity to see the play meaningfully is similarly, in the words of L. C. Knights, 'dependent upon our capacity to feel',[1] and why, moreover, critics generally seem to draw their own image when they try to say what the play really means. It is not that they read what is not actually there – in fact there are remarkably few who have not found something that *is* there and who have not obviously felt that this 'something' is given a special reality and significance by the play. It is rather that, in holding the mirror up to nature, the play enables and forces each of us to discover as its meaning only what our own individual, particular self can and must answer to in it.

---

[1] Knights, *Some Shakespearean Themes*, p. 117. Cf. Everett, 'The new *King Lear*', in Kermode (ed.), *Shakespeare: King Lear*, (Casebook Series), pp. 201–2.

III

For the characters in it, certainly, the world is not essentially ambiguous. (It is a different matter in *Macbeth* or *Antony and Cleopatra*, where that is the case.) Their objective world is 'nature', and although this may become ambiguous to us, for each of them it is manifold but determinable. 'Nature' is that which stands as objective to the perceiving self, the objects and forces each one has to acknowledge, within and without, as 'really there', since that is the very condition of possessing any specific sense either of his world or of himself. For none of the characters in *King Lear* is his self essentially an ambiguity, as it is for Hamlet. Each assumes he has a determinable identity; and perhaps the very common feeling that the characters in *King Lear* are especially simple, even monolithic, as personalities, largely comes from this pervasive assumption. Again, each character feels the need to realize his self – define it, assume responsibility for it, and act as moral agent; but if he can do so only in terms of what he sees as objective reality and knows as objective truth, none of them doubts that reality and truth are there to be found. Likewise, although we see that 'reality' is what each character can and must acknowledge as such, none of them doubts his ability to acknowledge it. None doubts that the world offers him the possibility of a definite meaning; on the contrary, we see that it actually does yield him one in so far as he acknowledges what it really consists in – that is, in so far as he *realizes* the nature of that world. And since it is a matter neither of illusion nor of solipsistic projection, 'realize' has to carry a double sense: fulfilling the self in an act of understanding, *and* thereby fulfilling nature.

But if 'nature's infinite book of secrecy', to use the

Soothsayer's phrase in *Antony and Cleopatra*, *is* a book, though realized as such only in being read, and men cannot choose but read it in order to realize themselves, it is also shown to yield none of its true meaning unless they also realize that its subject-matter includes themselves. Even while they have to accept that it exists apart from them in order to take it as a book, they also have to accept that they participate in the 'nature' they read, and it in them, in order to extract any adequate, or even specific, meaning from it. (No one seeks to read a nature he supposes is totally independent of human nature; that is virtually to define it as 'indifferent' or 'meaningless'.) As the play shows us again and again, for a man not to see, as *also* part of the nature he is reading, his own need as well as his capacity to read it as he does, is necessarily to read it inadequately and to realize his own self inadequately too. And yet, as the play also shows us, this is the one thing he can never see fully and still read any definite meaning in nature. If he could do so, he would indeed read it truly as an integral, coherent totality, and possess all of himself; but it would be a totality consisting of nothing less than all the possible ways it could be read, and a self consisting of every human possibility. To realize the full, ultimate meaning of nature – as his experience of it makes Lear feel he must, for example – would be to *see* nothing in particular and *be* no particular identity. In the end, his most basic need, the ultimate demand nature imposes, is for some unrealizable realization of it, some ungivable, or at least unformulable, answer; and perhaps it is the logic of this, inherent in the dramatic action, that leads some people to see the play as a religious one. It could obviously be taken as portraying or allegorizing the process wherein nature and man grope towards their eventual, transcendental salvation in God.

All the same, this is not how the play itself puts it. One way it does, though, is in terms of the 'justice' any man must want – the moral coherence, the meaning, to be found in reality – and the word 'justice' may properly remind us that the logic of the action as a whole inheres in each of its elements too. The interdependence of all its terms (if we can call them that) – self and nature, vulnerability and will, patience and action, ordering creation and destruction, energy and resistant form, one need and another, or, considering its artistic terms, one character and another, one scene or episode and another, one speech or image or word and another – does not diminish the particular, independent, competing identity of each one of those terms. Similarly, the activity of realizing their interdependence, and the activity of realizing their separate independence, are themselves dependent on each other – but that again does not make the activities any the less distinct. Each term and activity assumes its specific nature and shape precisely in being set beside its correlative. Neither Lear nor we can grasp the reality of Cordelia, for instance, without seeing some meaning embodied in the immediate living fact of her; and in the reconciliation scene, we cannot do that except by an answering integrity, harmony, and 'patience' of heart in ourselves. The meaning she bears in nature is, to that extent, *realized* – and the word now has to have a third sense, the poetic-dramatic, to complete the other two. Yet the integrity and harmony and patient love are visible to us only because they are bounded by the (at least) equal reality of incoherence, will, and conflict. These are visibly embodied in the world that Cordelia not merely inhabits but actually shares, just as they exist in the self with which Lear (and we) answer to that world. Hence the felt pressure in Lear (as in us) of yet a further need: to realize a more inclusive 'justice', a greater coherence, than even the particular reality of Cordelia offers in itself – even though her existence seems the only guarantee and the only image of its existence.

In other words, we need the meaning we see in Cordelia to prevail, to be *fully* realized in nature and in ourselves; and what is true here at the end is true everywhere else in the play. Whatever reality Lear acknowledges, for instance, though it is much the same for the other characters as well, always turns out to lack a full enough justice for him. Some part of reality always seems absent; some possibility of his self unrealized. Indeed, every human need in the play is shown to answer to a lack, an absence, a silence, a 'nothing', in the immediate world. For each character, to realize a need is to realize a gap in his present world, a gap whose shape has become visible only in what he acknowledges as real in that world, and which he then seeks to fill. For the 'nothing' now may be the possibility of an ultimate 'everything' (though if we consider it abstractly, this everything could never be realized as any thing at all), or it may be nothing indeed, an irreducible gap that finally denies any comprehensive meaning to the world and any comprehensive realization to the self. Hence the risk; and hence the fineness of the line, if there is a line, between 'everything' and 'nothing'.

Nevertheless, as we see over and over again, whenever a character seeks to act (physically or mentally) upon reality so as to make it answer to his need, his very action only serves to destroy one form of reality and one need by creating another. Like the effect of a 'green thought' on 'all that's made', each possibility is annihilated in the very moment it is realized in action. Nor can men ever escape the need to do this while they live on this side of the ultimate 'everything' they are impelled to seek. For Lear, say, or Edgar, or anyone else for that matter, the need may exist only as a continual pressure on him from within and without; but we know it to be a '*true* need' by the continual gap we realize between his sense of things and our own more complete one. We see, that is to say, how every answer he makes to his world requires still another, a fuller one if he can make it so, and that he can only realize his own life (and that of his world) by suffering the destruction of every particular form of it in another of its possibilities.

Lear's world can give him no realizable answer to his question: 'Why should a dog, a horse, a rat have life, / And thou no breath at all?' If the world does hold a reason why, how could he apprehend it? Yet the world forces the question on him and forces him to the question; indeed, it cannot yield him an answer just because the question issues from and expresses his very deepest sense of reality, as reality declares itself in the particular fact of this death. His question seeks nothing less than a total, irrefragable coherence, one encompassing every particular and every possibility; nothing less could be the meaning of *this* fact, since all the issues of life are now concentrated for him in grasping the meaning he feels in it. It is an 'extremity' to him because reducible to nothing else. Everything is at stake in it. Merely to be alive is to need to answer to the fact – somehow to possess (and to master) what completely possesses him. He therefore now has to acknowledge as real what had been too simple, too basic, too unimportant in itself for him (or anyone else) really to notice at all, even when he was most fully and freely aware. Only in relation to the life of any mere dog, or horse, or rat, can he realize the absence of Cordelia's life; yet it is only by finding no objective meaning in their lives that he can grope for some objective meaning in her death.

In the action, his question takes only a moment, of course, yet its note is so powerful that it is worth pausing to try to understand how and why. In part, its resonance comes, as I have tried to suggest, from the sheer 'extremities' it expresses. But another part comes from Lear's inability to take hold of a coherent, total reality in which the animals' living existence and Cordelia's death are equally and fully real and equally and fully meaningful. No sooner does he mention the beasts than his mind is immediately and wholly swamped by 'thou'. The only form in which he can grasp at the two together, in fact, is that of a question. For us, this is true in a parallel, but different way. For one instant, we can hold the question itself in our minds as an object – look at it as well as ask it – and because we can, we are almost able to realize the individual beasts' lives and Cordelia's death as equally real and equally part of a single coherent whole, one in which the life or death of every individual creature contains the same 'extremity' since the reality of one is the reality of all. This totality flashes into a sort of identifiable existence for us for that instant; we almost sense some ultimate coherence simultaneously with the incoherence of its particulars, as if the very form of the question contained its own answer; but then for us too it necessarily breaks apart into the discrete terms of the question: those things, this thing. Just as for Lear, the particular fact of Cordelia's death is so demanding and yet so hard to realize in full that it drains the particularity of 'a dog, a horse, a rat' away into a mere mental conception, possibilities the mind has no desire or capacity to realize at the moment.

Nevertheless, there is one fact it cannot drain away for us:

Lear's actual asking of the question. This is the only answer human nature *can* make to this extremity, and given the simple, basic, intractable, and immitigably painful fact to which it must answer, it can do so only from whatever is most simple, most basic, most unself-regarding, and most vulnerable in itself. In its dramatic context, what strikes us most about Lear's question is its direct, urgent simplicity – a simplicity of utterance that contrasts very markedly with the turbulent complexities earlier.[1] But just as the simplicity depends on the presence of the earlier complexities within it, as it were, for its power and value to us, so theirs depended upon its presence within them. The bare, direct nakedness of speech here marks both the fundamental inner extremity Lear is now driven to and the fundamental outer extremity that drives him there. It marks it as the vulnerable centre on which Lear's self has alway turned – though, as with a wheel, this has meant always turning away from it – and as the risk, the possibility of 'nothing', always latent in the external world that eventually gives it a real and therefore particular shape.

It may seem only a paradox to say that Lear's question is itself part of the only answer the world can make to Cordelia's death and therefore part of the meaning of the play – though if so, it is one much easier to state than to realize and accept. For Lear himself there is little chance of doing so. *We* can see it is only his love that makes the gap of Cordelia's death real and visible to him, and thereby forms the desperate, absolute need of his self to fill it with at least a meaning – an answering, objective, visible reason. Similarly, we can see it is only his absolute need of love that

[1] Winifred M. T. Nowottny makes some very pertinent observations about the style of the play in 'Lear's Questions', *Shakespeare Survey*, X (1957), and 'Some Aspects of the Style of *King Lear*', *Shakespeare Survey*, XIII (1960).

makes the gap too huge for any but a total answer to fill it – a visible cosmic justice. How could he see his very need and capacity to feel – which make her death real, and its injustice real, and both of them intolerable – are themselves the 'answer' reality offers to his question? As always, he can realize the 'heart' of his own being, the unprotectable vulnerability behind any regress or defence, only in the objects it needs, and which alone give his self any definable shape at all. Like anyone, he ultimately needs to experience the world (if we might put it in Buber's terms) both as 'It' and as 'Thou', since the two are interdependent. Nevertheless, there is a point at which they must break apart, and it is incalculable. In the reconciliation scene, for example, Cordelia did become a real 'Thou' to him because he could also fully acknowledge her as an independent reality. Here, too, he needs to acknowledge the full reality of her death and also to experience it as the world's address to *him*, as a 'Thou': the very form of his question, indeed, tries to bridge the world as 'It' and the world as 'Thou':

> Why should a dog, a horse, a rat, have life,
> And thou no breath at all

The struggle to bridge that gap *is* life, we may say, but so is realizing and accepting that it probably cannot be done; and it is a question, I think, which of them we really want Lear to achieve here. He can only grasp the full reality of Cordelia's death by suffering it nakedly, exposing the self to it completely; and he does. But at the same time he also needs to grasp it with his mind, consciously possess the sense of it; and he cannot do both. To be fully alive, alive *as* himself and *to* this fact, he has to surrender one to the other – which is totally to suffer; yet it is his very suffering that demands a justifying reason; and if such a reason would lessen the suffering, perhaps he needs that merely to survive in order to suffer the fact as justly as it deserves. It is no wonder he seems out of his mind. In fact some critics, I notice, describe him as 'mad', almost as if his state were one of mere defeat, and in that were somehow different from our own. But if he does not succeed and is not exactly sane – not at any rate as we use the word in ordinary life – what on earth can be meant by calling him mad? How, we may well ask, would a 'sane' man answer to Cordelia's death? But of course as soon as we ask that, we realize it would not be the exactly same fact if he did: the proof that she is really dead, and that her life really matters, is that no one could fully possess those facts and still be fully in possession either of himself or of the world. If sanity consists in seeing life truly and seeing it whole, *being* wholly and truly alive is the pretty un-sane condition of trying to achieve it.

IV

With Lear's state at the end here, and his final speech in particular, it is hard not to feel as Bradley did, that 'to dwell on [its] pathos . . . would be an impertinence'[1] – though dwelling on its pathos would certainly be preferable to the evasive, patronizingly sentimental 'poor-old-man: he's-better-off-dead' kind of impertinence. It is not just that decency and tact are called for; it is almost as if any words at all might violate what we see here – which is surely not pathos merely, but something rarer, more substantial, and even more vulnerable than that. Lear is utterly fragmented in the effort to answer to Cordelia's death, but his pathos can hardly be separated from his almost terrifying simplicity, nor these from the bare purity with which he is him-

[1] Bradley, *Shakespearean Tragedy*, p. 292.

self and himself alone, nor any of these finally from what we have to acknowledge in them: the elements of a *humanity* whose plight, and therefore whose authority (moral and dramatic authority), are absolute for us.

Although Lear still has an identity, a recognizable style even – his speeches could come from no one else, for example – it is an identity beyond any possible consciousness of itself. Moreover, it is virtually impossible for us to characterize it either: he now exists beyond the level of definable moral character altogether. The various forms in which his self has apprehended 'reality' while at the same time trying to render itself invulnerable to it – the moral categories and judgments, the aggressive-defensive will and actions and thoughts, the differing shapes, the continuous shaping – which together defined his particular identity to himself and to others, now, in as much as they made reality coherent, break apart; in as much as they protected him from it, they break open. What lies exposed is, in one aspect, only ruins; in the other, it is still a kind of self, one not any more real than its earlier forms, but certainly more basic. It is so basic indeed that it could not be defined in any less general terms than mere 'need' and bare 'capacity', were it not for the one particular reality these are now entirely directed to. As it is, we can describe him only as the limitless need and the limited capacity to realize *this*.

In other words, Lear does not now see or articulate, nor does his state merely exemplify, the fully and nakedly human; he *is* that. The capacity to speak, and to discover the reality of one's feelings and needs and circumstances (which is equally the capacity to distort or disguise them, of course), is an essential part of it. So is the inability ever to speak the whole of that reality. Similarly, the echo of his earlier unbuttoning in the storm-scene is an essential part of his last speech:

> . . . answer with thy uncover'd body this extremity of the skies
> . . . unaccommodated man is no more but such a poor, bare,
> forked animal as thou art. Off, off, you lendings! Come; unbutton
> here. (III, iv, 103ff)

> Pray you, undo this button: thank you, Sir. (v, iii, 309)

The difference goes beyond that 'thank you', unique though
it is for Lear. If the spirit of this line derives from the same
source as 'I know thee well enough; thy name is Gloucester' and 'as I am a man, I think this Lady/To be my child
Cordelia', it is significant that here he does not realize who
the particular 'Sir' he turns to is, and that it does not matter.
Likewise, his humanity does not now prove itself more than
the 'poor, bare, forked animal' by the very need to lacerate
his nature and assert that it is no more, and then tearing the
accommodating clothes from his body to satisfy the need.
It is visible in his now unreflected but acknowledgeable need
of help, of any human-kindness, of another's 'heart' as it
were, to free his own heart of its accommodating clothes – a
need realized to us here in his quiet acknowledgment even
of the button itself as a fact, and in the poor, bare, forked
animal's extremest need, to answer now with his bare
human self to another 'nothing'.

There is more than pathos in this final speech, in fact,
just because it embodies something more than Lear's individual character, no matter whether we want to call that
character 'redeemed' or not. What defines his identity
defines his humanity. It consists in his complete vulnerability to his own love, which is the realization, the hardest
possible realization, of the very medium of time in which it
lives but which inevitably destroys its object: 'never, never,
never, never, never!'; *and* in his particular need for total,
objective 'meaning', a cosmic justice, to cover that vulner-

ability, a need formed in the hardest realization of what can yield no meaning in so far as it is regarded as totally objective: 'Why should a dog, a horse, a rat have life?'; *and* in his particular need to act upon the world so as to make an answer in it, a need formed in the hardest, perhaps impossible, realization of what remains unchangeably silent: 'look on her, look, her lips'. Each of these is not so much dependent on the others as a particular aspect of them, but none can exist except in its own distinct, particular shape. For such a condition as this, 'redeemed' is surely too personal and too salvationist a word, unless it also means that he is so intensely, so openly, alive to his world that he shatters with the impact – or rather with the irresistible need to experience what nobody can: the irreducible reality of *everything* inside and outside the self. All through the action he has been king and hero in being so fully (which also includes in so particular, so individual, a way) a man. Unlike the others, his self has always been unabated – though not, being human, unconditioned or unlimited – in its sense of its own potentialities, in its will, needs, and demands. His sheer power to confront and if possible master his world has also been the power to be confronted and mastered by it. Here, in reaching its extremity, that self is still unabated: there is, we notice, no tendency to mere melancholy in his grief, absolutely no wish for, or gesture towards, a self-protective oblivion as in Gloucester. If the spectacle 'affirms' anything, it is perhaps only the indissoluble reality of the world that can bring him to this, and the irreducible humanity that can suffer itself to be brought to it.

V

But Lear's is still not the whole reality the play puts before

178

us. Our reality includes the world Lear sees, and him seeing it, and the other characters who see these too. 'Look on her, look' – but as well as Cordelia's body, we also see the two other circles of awareness concentric with ours. The world that realizes itself in this death and in the meaning the death finds in Lear's life can also realize itself as it does to Kent, or Edgar, or Albany. Everything, including the spectacle of Lear struggling with it, forces each of them to answer to it with his own naked self; as we see, the world is still capable of the shape Kent characteristically finds in it – 'Break, heart; I prithee, break' . . . 'the rack of this tough world'; or Edgar – 'Look up, my Lord'; or Albany – 'Rule in this realm, and the gorg'd state sustain'; or by extension, any of the others.

Naturally it is very tempting to deny this last possibility. Endings look so conclusive; and even if no single right view of things is left, that does not mean that there are not wrong ones, and some, it may seem, have been conclusively revealed as that. But wrong to whom? Wisdom and goodness to the vile still seem vile; how could an Albany, for instance, ever make Goneril acknowledge her vileness?

> GON. Say, if I do, the laws are mine, not thine:
> Who can arraign me for't? . . .
>   Ask me not what I know.   (v, iii, 158ff)

She is a far tougher proposition than Iago, and unfortunately there is nothing that can deny a Goneril her own possible view of the last scene ('An interlude!') – nothing, that is, except her defeat and death. But after all, what do defeat and death prove about Cordelia? We cannot have it both ways, even though (as reasonable beings) we want to. Evil has not been decisively expelled from the world of the action; indeed, it has not even been decisively isolated.

Although moral evil is defeated, its consequence – the natural evil (as it must seem) of Cordelia's death – is only the other face of the defeat, and that remains. Or to put the point another way, the basic, shattering reality of:

Never, never, never, never, never!

does *not* dissolve the equally basic, shattering reality of, say:

Then, kill, kill, kill, kill, kill, kill!

As with the picture-puzzle, so with any great work of art: the particulars remain obstinately themselves. Whatever whole we actually grasp must be *less* than the sum of its parts; the losses involved in any total 'meaning' have no remedies.

We might well see the meaning of *King Lear* as precisely that. Time and again the characters are seen trying to hold reality and justice in a single thought, yet every attempt visibly fails because of some crucial loss in one or the other term. In the end the action may come to seem something like a paradigm of the necessities, the 'needs', conditioning the effort to make reality yield any meaning at all. If we do regard the play in this way, then perhaps the critical oscillation about it, between those for whom it is bearable because they discern some definable meaning in it and those for whom it is not, is a paradigm of everyone's personal situation at the end. We seem to swing dizzily between these two possibilities – until we choose (as we feel we must) between them.

Up to a point, I think this is the case; and putting it in these terms may help to clarify how *Antony and Cleopatra* could be said to follow naturally (if unpredictably) from the very different issues and spirit of *King Lear*. But it is surely only up to a point – for even this view of the play fails to meet the case for exactly the same reasons as prompt it. We do not *experience* the play as a paradigm, a design illustrating the possibilities of making sense of life and the impossibility of ever making total sense of it. We experience it rather in its particulars: as this sense, and that sense, in this man's experience and that man's experience of this, and this. . . . The poetry and deeds that constitute the action make the possibilities and the losses real to us; and the point is that they are real, and really matter, only in the particular substance of individual human lives.

In trying to take full and just possession of our dramatic experience, therefore, we have to acknowledge the reality we experience remains, as it must, open. It never closes in to some fully guaranteed true 'insight' or 'vision'. The vision it offers us resides in the fate of human figures whose limitations of insight, as we see, are not only essential to their humanity but actually *are* their fate. And to see this is thereby to acknowledge that our own insight, although larger, is necessarily limited too (as is Shakespeare's, for that matter). However helpful it may be to regard the play as a 'dramatic poem', it is dramatic in more than form. Being composed of human figures, its very mode tacitly eschews the claim to, or even the possibility of, any unquestionable vision – whether moral, philosophical, religious, or prophetic. Indeed, in so far as drama must exhibit in some way or another the inevitability of human error, it must retain a proper spiritual modesty for itself; it has a necessary final scepticism built in, as it were, which becomes more important an element of its meaning precisely as the work is more fully dramatic in its form and substance. For this reason we may prefer, say, Dante to Shakespeare; personally, I think it is a reason for preferring Shakespeare (if we have to prefer either); but in any case, it is not a reason to try to assimilate Shakespeare's kind of art to Dante's. *King Lear*, for instance, is not the expression or the 'affirmation' of some moral or metaphysical or epistemological truth or of the ultimate supremacy of some particular value – love, understanding, honesty, energy, feeling, or even ambiguity.

On the other hand, it must (like any drama) both exhibit and engage such values. As we try to comprehend our dramatic experience, we have no less to acknowledge that we could not experience anything unless our moral values were engaged in particular acts of judgment, sympathy, hope, desire, and so on. Right from the beginning, the action involves us, at the very least, in understanding how these figures *are* human beings; as it proceeds, of course, it involves a good deal more of us than that. To return for a moment to the view that a Goneril might possibly take of the ending, for example, we could only say of it, as L. C. Knights pointed out, that such an attitude would be 'inhuman', and we could quite legitimately point to the whole action in support of our judgment. If the action makes any sense to us at all, then a Goneril-like view of the ending must be a kind of self-sustained (and no doubt self-sustaining) brutality. But the actual affirmation here is ours, not the play's. The trouble with trying to apply a word like 'affirmation' to the work is that we seem to want of it some final, comprehensive and therefore true *judgment*, some specific, very large, but fully authenticated 'criticism of life', as the sign of its imaginative greatness. In fact, the sign of its greatness is to give us instead something larger and more authentic, but finally incompatible with that: an image of the reality we share with each other and the characters, an image whose validity as such we have to acknowledge in the experience of it, and in the acknowledging bring the substance of our own selves to active life. We may rejoice that we *can* acknowledge it as such; in any case, we are too active to be depressed. It is not the whole substance of our selves, of course, as it is of the characters' – there are innumerable other 'horizons' (to use Wilson Knight's word) that we can and do acknowledge – but in this play it is at least some basic, bed-rock form of the self. Nor is it to 'self-knowledge' that the play brings us, to see and know this or that as the form of our self. Although the play elicits the form and leaves us vibrantly and painfully alive, we do not see our selves, any more than Lear can see his; we see only what we acknowledge as objectively real.

In this sense, the play yields us not a pre-established nor even an emergent judgment, but something more like an implicit yet gradually clarifying *norm* of judgment – a norm that exists in the only way such a norm could, namely as it is realized in a process, in action. The objective correlative of this action in us is the dramatic action – an intense, complex image, which necessarily moves in time. In terms of that, we can at least say why we choose to call Goneril 'inhuman' – what sort of thing it means to do so, and (equally important) what sort of thing it does not mean. For the basic human capacity we share with her, which is what enables us to judge her, is also what prompts us to do so and provides the terms in which we would: how she answers to the possibilities of life, what she acknowledges. It is less a matter of her 'character', her conscious moral disposition, will and habits, than of her personal identity itself – the ways in which, and the limits within which, she can feel and want and see at all. These underlie and shape both her 'character' and the 'reality' it takes itself to inhabit; her identity realizes itself in the ways each of these answers to the other. The limits of her capacity to feel for others or even with them, for instance, mark how little reality she can bear to acknowledge. If the world yields her a very clear-cut kind of meaning, so that for her 'justice' is a sharply definable state of affairs, and her sense of her own objective identity and power is correspondingly clear-cut, the cost is an incapacity to realize more identity and power than that. Like anyone else, she continuously chooses the terms on which she will risk herself, but hers are so sharp and narrow that they leave her a correspondingly brittle kind of security. She wants to win the whole kingdom and fears nothing to do so, not despite but because she fears so much. She can afford to surrender only very little of herself. Hence the paradox that some critics have noted, that could she have risked more (in fearing Lear less, for instance) she might have succeeded in her plot – though of course the terms on which she *is* herself are the only ones in which 'success' or 'failure' are real to her. The essential point is not therefore that she is foiled; it is not even the subtler nemesis, that she can finally see no way to protect her self but to murder it. It is rather that, while she is right and nothing can make her say 'what she knows', we actually know what she knows, and since it has never amounted to much (though it was something), we have already 'arraigned' her. We did so, and had to, in the hovel with Lear, for example, even while we did also, and had to, reserve ourselves from *his* precise terms ('Then, kill, kill, kill').

Similarly, we have had to realize and judge (though again nothing would ever prove) Kent's or Edgar's or Albany's views as inadequately human too: as betraying, that is, their incapacity to be more than the particular selves they settle for. Similarly, we have also had to realize that this is the very condition on which they are themselves.

As with Gloucester, so with them: such an incapacity at
some point or another is necessary to be a human being at
all. The same applies to Cordelia, or to the servant who kills
Cornwall, or the servant who helps the blinded Gloucester:
it is an incapacity to be more *or* less than the particular self
one can bear to be. To satisfy his 'true needs', each character
has to 'choose' how far his vulnerability to life extends,
what possibilities in himself and in the world he cannot risk
and so has to exclude. And as we see, Edgar is quite right:
because no one can really know how much of his own
identity he can bear to risk, men must be patient enough to
learn; and since the action places us in the same situation,
there are good reasons why many people should find the
play's meaning in 'ripeness is all'. Nevertheless, to be completely patient is to be dead; and reasonable though it is to
read the play as preaching patience from end to end, it
would not be at all unreasonable to read it the other way
around (as perhaps it is in some unusually literate under-
ground circle), as preaching heroic activism from end to
end. Lear's kingship and heroism, which are fully realized
only in the moment of his death, are defined by – but they
are also the measure and the sanction of – all the others'
more limited humanity. His reveals what it might bear at
its fullest pitch ('fullest' at least in the sense of most intensely naked); it also reveals the need and the incapacity
of any individual to realize everything and go on living.
Thus it is not moral 'character' that is fate so much as
identity – the particular limits that enable a being to think
and feel and will at all. And it is not so much 'fate' in the
ordinary sense of the word, as the limited possibilities of
our common world that are 'chosen' by a particular self
and thereby realized as it answers to them – or from another
point of view, those possibilities of our common life that

seem to reach out for a particular form in which to realize themselves. For all its unique power and economy, *King Lear* is clearly related to *Othello*, say, with its (admittedly more limited) interest in the way 'reality' coheres or breaks with the self, and to *Macbeth*, with its intenser concentration on the basic conditions in which identity is possible at all, as well as to *Antony and Cleopatra*, with its wider-ranging, metamorphic sense of our reality at its 'fullest'.

In focusing the possibilities of his own world, the hero's life becomes the objective focus of similar possibilities in ours. The last scene of *King Lear* brings us to a state analogous to Lear's own, although unlike him, unlike even the other characters who regard him, we also understand something of its necessity. We are quickened by similar needs to similar questions, even though we confront a world that also includes him as an object in it. Like him, we are impelled to confront it only because what we confront is not *merely* an object to our consciousness. The same interdependence of reality, meaning, and self that we see within the play applies to our relationship with what we acknowledge as the dramatic reality. That interdependence in the characters' experience – which is, as we have seen, rather like a closed system, until it is jolted open – has formed a total experience for us which, as we grasp its shape, forms a similarly closed system. It is not only a system of moral expectation and moral justice. The ubiquitous web of parallels and echoes, the simple but remorseless logic of events, the oppositions continually realized in identities and identities in oppositions, the ironies that turn reflexively back on themselves, the taut economy of the action, the measured thrust of its 'argument': all of this creates a world that seems wholly substantial and securely meaningful in its reality, until it is likewise jolted open. We suffer this last *peripeteia* for ourselves as well as sympathetically experiencing the characters' suffering of it. And the chaos we 'see', which we have to search again for meaning, and the possible shape we now have to find, are the correlatives of what we now are. We look for an answering 'justice' in the play so urgently just because our experience of it as real has made us as vulnerable to it as Lear is to his. I think our state even quickens the same impulse to action in us as we see in Lear's 'look there, look there!' – what else did Tate do, for instance, but make the dramatic reality answer to this need, while paying the inevitable cost of course? Indeed, we may well consider Johnson's inability to go on looking at what he saw (like Lear's inability to do so) as testifying to the depth of *his* humanity. So too with Bradley's feeling that words could hardly be found for the experience of Lear hardly able to find words for his: dwelling on his pathos would violate not only Lear's, but our own humanity too.

To say that *King Lear* gives us something like a norm of human vitality therefore requires some necessary qualifications. One is that it cannot be comprehended in any specific judgment. Another is that it is essentially tragic in the necessary incapacity of any specific life to sustain it either[1] – though obviously this fact offers a 'comic' side as well. (Hence the 'grotesque' aspects Wilson Knight has

[1] Something like this, I take it, is what Paul J. Alpers means when he says that 'we cannot separate Lear's terrible energies and moral demands from those that confer value on Cordelia and enable him to love her; nor can we propose a definition of "human" that includes Cordelia and excludes her sisters. The tragedy lies in the inevitability with which human experience will destroy anyone who tries to comprehend it all. And the tragedy is so stark and vast because it fully honors Lear's mode of experience. No image of individual man is available to us by which we can say it could or should be otherwise' ('King Lear and the Theory of the "Sight Pattern"', in Brower and Poirier (eds.), *In Defense of Reading*, p. 152).

pointed to in *King Lear*. Hence too, I think, the effort to comprehend both the comic and the tragic sides at once in the 'wit' of *Antony and Cleopatra*.) Again, we acknowledge its reality as a norm only in so far as we experience it inwardly, as a possibility that we truly need, and might even be able, to realize: that is to say, in so far as it is *truly* imagined, but also in so far as it is *only* imagined. We can realize it only in the medium of, and by our openness to and dependence upon, the felt reality of 'nature' and of other people; and yet the more fully and intensely we feel that reality, the less we can support what we realize. In other words, it would be more than an impertinence to dwell on the naked reality of Lear's last speech; it is an impossibility. All we can dwell on are those things about it that perhaps help explain the impossibility.

They may also help explain why the figure of Cordelia almost inevitably seems vital in some way to the meaning of the whole, as if something *had* been affirmed in her. It hasn't in fact – not in any ordinary sense; but she has imaged for us the fine (but impossible) balance, the full (but impossible) comprehension, with which, for a precarious but vibrant moment, we do seem to experience reality – a reality at once the world's and our own. In that, I think, and the image of it reflected in Cordelia (though only for a moment or two, and only partially), lies the 'sense of beauty' Bradley spoke of; in our realization of why and how it is impossible to sustain it, I think, lies the 'sense of law'. For we do seem to hold in our grasp, or rather to have held for a brief moment, or at least to be capable of holding, every possibility of reality without loss of any – except, that is, as we come to realize, the vital one entailed by the fact that we experience it only in, and by means of, a dramatic fiction.

The fiction does speak the truth, of course, and like that of Cordelia's 'no cause, no cause', it is not merely about the heart, but of the heart. The most difficult thing of all is to speak both together, and one of the triumphs of the play is to do just that. It does so even in the last, brief 'choric' speeches. The penultimate word is given to Kent – 'My master calls me, I must not say no' – and our feelings answer in assent to his, even while we are detached enough to see how the speech as *he* means it answers to the pathos of his particular self. Almost every one of his words has a meaning for us as real as, but still different from, its meaning to him. The same applies to the last speech too, though here the voice is still further removed from the immediacy of all we have experienced:

> The weight of this sad time we must obey;
> Speak what we feel, not what we ought to say.
> The oldest hath borne most: we that are young
> Shall never see so much, nor live so long.

If we can still attend to this while it is said, we must assent to it. We too 'must obey' the 'weight'; we too must feel 'young' and inadequate even to see or to live so much; and it hardly matters whether it is Edgar's voice who says this for us or (as the Quarto has it) Albany's. Yet who but Edgar would be ready with 'philosophical' reflections to the very last – and with such a characteristically impossible precept as 'speak what we feel'? Bradley calls Edgar's character 'religious', and there is no denying that he is rather given to fine sentiments. On the other hand, it is no doubt something to have learned that 'what we feel' is not the same as 'what we ought to say', and that one may be more important than the other.

But as usual Edgar is a little beside the point, for we need to speak not merely what we feel, but also, along with that, what we see. Moreover, as Cordelia showed at the beginning, it is not easy to distinguish between what we feel and what we ought to say. The mere fact of having to speak can so easily compromise the integrity of feeling we try to express. Not only can words be misunderstood and betray our intended meaning; our very consciousness of self almost inevitably betrays the self. What Edgar ought to say, therefore, is 'speak what we really are, not what we think we are' – though of course this is not quite what *he* has come to feel or what he thinks he now sees. Nor, even if it were, could he or anyone else really 'speak' it. If we could grasp everything we have experienced, and express it coherently and with complete justice to the experience, we could thereby bear it all – even bear something away from it. As with Lear so with us: the need to know and thus to master everything meets only the impossibility of doing so; and the impossibility is the need finally to answer to everything with the whole of the self and yet to know, or to utter, or to see, or to feel, or to love – in short, to be – something particular. In the end, I do not believe we can define the state of heightened vitality to which the play brings us. If we did not acknowledge the dramatic reality as our own, we could not be brought to that state; if we did not acknowledge the dramatic reality as fictitious, not actually our own, we could not support the state. We realize the substances and values of our life, our 'bonds', in answering to the play's life – whether in a dog or a mere button, in the flashes of lightning, in the ambiguous voice of the thunder, in each particular human 'heart', in each horror, love, suffering, and death; yet we could not 'see so much', and speak what we see, unless we needed to answer to it, really answer to it in our own selves, only for a moment and provisionally – with a crucial, but still open question, as it were.

As I see it then, the critic (being after all only a member of the audience who does dwell impertinently on the experience of the play in the hope of saying what it is) eventually reaches the same point in the terms of his own activity as Lear exhibits in his. While needing to do nothing less than realize the whole of his experience as meaningful, he can do nothing more than gather what sense he can of its question, and say finally only, 'look there, look there!' No critical 'saying', I think, can be final, because no one can experience as a coherent, final judgment all the possibilities of judgment the play evokes. No particular 'answering' can comprehend every form the question can, indeed must, assume for other individuals. On the other hand, it is impossible not to answer to the play, and to do so is necessarily to 'speak' something definite: even something as open as this. But if the 'weight' of the action – the felt substance and density of its life – does force each of us to 'obey' and speak (though not necessarily in words, of course), at least it doesn't violate *our* humanity. It enables as immensely as it forces: it allows, that is, each of us the freedom to 'speak' our own particular, though common, human existence.

Having reached this point with the play – defining these particular limits to its meaning – a critic has obviously reached the point where he has to surrender: beyond this, the light of critical sense goes out completely. Still, criticism can retire with relative grace. The producer – like Nahum Tate – has no such solution; and although I began by questioning what producers have sometimes done with *King Lear*, I think their predicament is instructive. The producer must finally settle for some one definite but comprehensive sense of a play in order to realize both it and his own function in the real world. He has to 'speak' the whole drama in a specific form, while yet respecting (if he thinks of it) the freedom of the drama and of each member of the audience to answer to each other in different ways. *King Lear* presents that problem very acutely (more so, I think, than any other Shakespearean tragedy – even *Antony and Cleopatra*). On the one side there is Lamb's view: 'Lear is essentially impossible to be represented on a stage.' If we make that *King Lear*, Lamb undoubtedly has a point. Yet can we really take it as a conclusive one? After all, is it not only human, as we might say, to *want* to speak, to act, to come together, and actually 'see so much, and live so long'? – 'Life delights in life'.